Christ for Real

How to Grow into God's Likeness

Charles W. Price

kregel
PUBLICATIONS

Grand Rapids, MI 49501

Christ for Real: How to Grow into God's Likeness
by Charles W. Price.

Originally published in English by Marshall Pickering, an imprint of HarperCollinsPublishers Ltd. The author asserts the moral right to be identified as the author of this work.

© 1995 by Charles W. Price.

Published in 1995 by Kregel Publications, a division of Kregel, Inc., P.O. Box 2607, Grand Rapids, MI 49501.

Scripture quotations, unless otherwise noted, are from *The Holy Bible: The New International Version* copyright © 1978 by the International Bible Society. Used by permisson of Zondervan Bible Publishers.

Library of Congress Cataloging-in-Publication Data
Price, Charles W. (Charles Wesley), 1949–
    Christ for Real: How to Grow into God's Likeness/
Charles W. Price.
        p.   cm.
    Originally published: London: Marshall Pickering, 1985.
    1. Salvation. 2. Sanctification. 3. Image of God. 4.
Christian life. I. Title.
BT752.P75   1995   234—dc20   94-48415
                                                                                    CIP
ISBN 978-0-8254-3550-8

                8 9 10 11 Printing/Year 11 10 09 08

                Printed in the United States of America

Contents

Acknowledgments

I was twelve years of age when I first met Major Ian Thomas. At the end of one of his meetings in the Town Hall in Hereford, I asked him to sign his name in my New Testament. He wrote, "All that God is, you have. You cannot have more, you do not need to have less." I didn't understand the full meaning of those words at the time, but I am deeply grateful to God for all that I learned from Major Thomas in the following years, as his life and ministry taught me what it means to be a true Christian. It was a special joy to have been invited by Major Thomas to join the team at Capernwray Hall and to become part of a group of people, operating in many countries of the world, for whom I hold the deepest respect, love, and admiration. So many of the truths in this book I have learned with and from these people. I am especially grateful to Dr. Alan Redpath, who for many years was a colleague at Capernwray Hall, for his kindness in writing a foreword to the book.

My gratitude must be expressed to John Hunt of Marshall Morgan and Scott, who initiated this book and who gave me much encouragement in the early days of its formation. I am grateful, too, to Alan Matthews, managing director of Bagster Video, who sowed the first seeds in John Hunt's mind.

Finally, my deepest thanks go to my wife, Hilary, for her encouragement, her reading of the manuscript at its various stages of development, and the many, many valuable suggestions and corrections! This has been written during a busy year. Parts of the manuscript have traveled in my briefcase to such places as Japan, New Zealand, Australia, and the U.S.A., in most cases returning exactly as they left. This has meant that nearly all the real work on this book took place at home, and I am more grateful than I can say to Hilary for her willingness to let me come home after several weeks away and spend most of my time shut away in my study to work on this book. It is to her credit that it is now completed.

Forewords

At my time of life, one is constantly looking over one's shoulder to see what men are coming along who preach not themselves, but Jesus Christ, crucified and risen, to be Lord and not only Savior. I have known the author of this book for many years and have always had the deepest regard and affection for him. Undoubtedly he is one of those to whom I refer. The Lord has His hand upon him, not least because he has always emphasized that the introduction to a vital relationship with Christ involves genuine repentance which enables faith to be valid.

This book confirms that and more, for it is a solid biblical exposition from beginning to end of the sovereignty of our Lord Jesus Christ and His demand for Christian revolution as the basis of a relationship with Him. In other words, if we pray, "Thy kingdom come," we must first pray, "My kingdom go." This aspect of the gospel is so often missing in methods of evangelism which attempt to reach others by entertainment rather than a clear-cut exposition of Scripture. This book deserves a wide readership, and it will be especially helpful to small groups seeking to grow together in the knowledge of God and His Word, as well as for individual readership and study.

It has been a privilege to write the foreword to this, his first book, which I am sure will not be his last.

ALAN REDPATH

Charles Price is a young British preacher whose ministry has been increasingly appreciated in many parts of the world. His accent betrays his roots in the beautiful west country of England, and his content demonstrates his roots in the wonderful Word of God. His ready wit and warm humor make listening to him easy, while his practical application and apt illustrations make him profitable and challenging. He comments simply but not superficially. He is theological without being tedious or contentious.

In an age when even Christianity is in danger of becoming man-centered, Charles Price insists on being Christ-centered. If this sounds impractical, read him. You will find that anecdotes abound proving he knows how to show people that Christ is for real and for real people.

STUART BRISCOE

In this clearly written and helpfully illustrated book, Charles Price strips away the evangelical myths that have overgrown the Gospel and challenges us to stop trying to live for Jesus and start discovering Christ who is our life, the only true source of spiritual victory and reality. It ought to be required reading for all Christians. I gladly commend it.

DOUG BARNETT

1

Being the Christian
You Have Become

Have you ever tried to get hold of a piece of soap in the bath? No sooner is it in your hand, than it has slipped from your grasp and is gone again! For many people their Christian experience has seemed to treat them like that. There has been the new thrill of discovering Jesus Christ to be alive and relevant. There is excitement in learning some new truth about His purpose and ability to bring quality and meaning into the normal routine of life. There is the exhilaration of a fresh experience of God that at last gives hope of consistency and vitality. But no sooner does it seem in their grasp than it has slipped away again, leaving behind only a memory and a feeling of hopelessness. Staring them in the face is the frustration of having been unable to maintain momentum and the underlying fear that things will perhaps never change. Do you know what I am talking about?

The first years of my Christian life fitted that description well. I became sure of my salvation one Saturday evening in the town hall in Hereford, where I had gone to see a dramatic film, the main character of which had been converted to Christ through a Billy Graham crusade in Australia. The town hall was full that night. I was unable to obtain a seat, so I stood along the side for the full two hours or so of the evening's program. As the story unfolded, I was spellbound. Based in the Australian outback, the film probed into the life of a man who was discovering his need for Christ, and although there was nothing in common between my life and his, I became especially aware of my own need. As far as the message of the film was concerned, I was not hearing anything that was new in its content, for I had heard it often before, but it was new in its vitality and fresh in its relevance. I knew God was speaking to me, and that I had to make a response. An opportunity was given after the showing for those who wanted help or counsel to come to the front of the hall. As others went, I remained where I was. It seemed too public and I was shy. I just didn't know at this stage whether I was a Christian or not, for I had known and believed the Gospel since being very young, but as others went to the front to find help, I remember praying very simply, "Lord Jesus Christ, if I am not a Christian, please make me one tonight." I went home that night with an assurance I had not known before, and which I have never doubted since. I was a Christian. Of that I was now sure, although all that that meant was not to become real to me for several more years. But for now, there was a new love in my heart for God, a new desire to please Him, and a new attitude to people and life in general.

However, this is where the problems started, for the very change of attitude and desire, the new ambitions to live for God and to please Him, made me acutely aware of how far short the reality of my life fell below the ideals that I longed to hold in my grasp. My joy and my enthusiasm soon turned to frustration. Although I did not dare admit it fully, my Christianity did not work and I was a failure. I neither knew nor would have understood the verse at that time which states, "For it is God who works in you to will and to act according to His good purpose" (Phil. 2:13). I was discovering a new "will" that was unmistakably God-given, for my desires and ambitions had changed. But I did not know that God was to be equally involved in fulfilling the "act," and in my obvious weakness I struggled to bring my behavior pattern into consistency with what I willed. And it was the difference between the will to do right and the act that was the measure of my frustration.

Well-meaning preachers often added to my helplessness by challenging me to a greater "dedication" to Christ. With genuine sincerity I would solemnly dedicate myself. Feeling this had been a good step, a fresh zeal would return, there would seem a new spring in my step and a vision of truly getting somewhere this time. But within days I would be back where I had started. Soon I would be challenged again to "rededicate" myself to God. I cannot recall how many times I went through that process, and every time with utmost sincerity. Like the elusive soap in the bath, so often I thought I had gotten a hold on it, but it never lasted.

After a while it was hard to know what I was really looking for.

Were my sights too high? To be honest, it didn't seem that many of the Christians I knew were living as they should, although I did know a few who were. Were the standards of the Bible unrealistic? Did God give an extra high standard in order to motivate us to keep pressing on, but which it would be unwise to take too literally? If that were so, it would appear that God was teasing us by dangling fantastic promises like a carrot in front of a donkey's nose, knowing that every time we moved toward them they would always remain just out of reach.

The dawning of hope began with a discovery. In retrospect it was a discovery which could hardly seem to be more simple or more obvious. It could hardly have been more obvious because the very terminology I was familiar with in describing the Christian life contained the truth I had failed to take literally or appreciate as the essence of Christian experience. It was simply this: Jesus Christ had come to live in me. Had you asked me if Christ was in me, I would have replied "Yes," but in practice He was like a silent partner who played no active role now that He had saved me from the penalty of my sin and set me on the road to heaven.

TICKET, CERTIFICATE, AND CATALOG

Until this time Christ was to me only the patron of my Christianity, rather than its life. It was in His name that we were to live, but not in His strength. I thought of myself as having received certain things from Christ that had enabled me to become a Christian and were my provision for trying to live the Christian life. Basically there were three things: a ticket, a certificate, and a catalog.

The "ticket" stated: "One way journey to heaven." I knew that this was a vital part of the whole arrangement. Through the acknowledgment of my sin before God and my willingness to turn from it, I had an assurance of the gift of eternal life. I was going to heaven. I believed that this was the ultimate goal of the work of Christ, the reason why He had died and the object of my salvation.

The "certificate" stated: "This is to certify that Charles Price has had all his sins forgiven . . . signed, God." This was absolutely necessary in order for me to be eligible for the ticket. Furthermore, the certificate had been written in blood, for the Bible stated, "The blood of Jesus, his son, purifies us from every sin" (1 John 1:7). My life now was surely to be a response to this, by living in such a way that I was expressing gratitude for all He had done.

Of course, it was the living for Him that was so difficult, and it was to enable me to do this that I had been given the third item, a "catalog." It was called the Bible. I imagined God to be in heaven with a great supermarket with its shelves stacked high with spiritual goodies. With Him was someone I imagined to fulfill the role of an errand boy and who was called the Holy Spirit. How all this operated was very simple. I was to read the catalog and discover all the things that were available to me from God and then through prayer to put in my order, and it would be the task of the Holy Spirit to bring these various commodities to me. For example, on reading the catalog I discovered I could have "love." Having then prayed and asked God to give me some, I imagined the Holy Spirit coming with a tube of love (I imagined it being like toothpaste) and squeezing it all over my emotions so that I would become loving. It might seem to last for a little while and was nice while it did! Then, on reading the Bible, I would discover I could have "joy." Feeling a little miserable, I would ask for some joy, and I thought of the Holy Spirit coming to me with a bottle of joy (I pictured this as like a bubble bath mixture) and after giving it a good shake would pour it all over my mind and emotions and I would become joyful! One of my greatest needs was for power, and I would plead with God to send me power so that I could serve Him properly, and I imagined the Holy Spirit being sent with a stick of power, lighting the blue fuse and standing back while I exploded with a new power for a while. Of course, none of these things were lasting, and there would be the need to keep coming back to the supermarket for more. It was tiring, and always, always short-lived.

But now I was seeing that God was not giving me things or showering upon me a wide range of spiritual commodities. God was giving me HIMSELF. All the things I had asked for were to be an expression of the life of God within me. It was to be the active presence and working of God Himself within my life that made the Christian life possible. It was no longer to be a case of me living down here for a God who, to all intents and purposes, was still living up there. Rather it was to be a release of the Holy Spirit within me, that He might live the life of Jesus Christ, reproducing the character of Jesus Christ and reflecting the likeness of Jesus Christ in all of the ordinary and mundane details of life. What was needed on my part was not so much a dedication to live for God, but a dying to myself and to self-sufficiency, coupled with a reliance upon God "to will and to act according to his good pleasure." Paul wrote to the Corinthians, "For we who are alive are always being given over to death for Jesus' sake, so that *His life* may be revealed in our mortal body" (2 Cor. 4:11).[1]

DEDICATION OR DEATH?

Some of the sad events in the Bible are in the lives of people who, rather than letting God do His work, dedicated themselves to doing things for Him. Sometimes the greater the sincerity of their dedication, the sadder the story. Let me give examples from two of the most significant men in the Old Testament.

When Abraham was at the ripe old age of seventy-five and his wife Sarah ten years his junior, God gave him a remarkable promise. Surveying the stars in the sky and the sand on the seashore, he was told his descendants would be as numerous as they. The only problem was that Abraham and Sarah had been married for many years, had failed to produce any children, and all hope of doing so had long died. But, because it was God who said it, they believed it, and with great anticipation and joy they waited . . . and waited . . . and waited! Ten years passed by. Abraham was now eighty-five and Sarah seventy-five, but there was still no child. This was an acute embarrassment to them as well as a tragic disappointment. What should they do? What could they do? In Genesis 16 there is recorded their conversation together about this and their subsequent plan of action. Abraham would father a child through the maidservant Hagar. This was not an alien practice within their culture, several other men in Genesis also having produced children through their wives' servants. It was never sanctioned by God, of course, but it did take place. Abraham consequently took Hagar and she conceived and gave birth to a baby boy whom they called Ishmael.

Abraham's motivation was sincere. He had given up all hope of having a child until God spoke to him. Now with the promise of God ringing in his ears for the past ten years, he dedicated himself to doing the will of God. Ishmael was not conceived in an act of rebellion against God but in an attitude of agreement with God. It was not out of disobedience, but out of a dedication to God's purpose that Abraham and Sarah had planned the means whereby Ishmael might be born. But God did not recognize Ishmael. It was another

---

1. italics mine throughout

fourteen years after Ishmael was born that Sarah herself conceived and gave birth to Isaac, a full twenty-five years after the promise had been given. Later when God tested Abraham and asked him to offer Isaac in sacrifice, He referred to Isaac as "your only son" (Gen. 22:2). God did not recognize Ishmael, as He does not recognize our efforts on His behalf, no matter how sincerely they have been carried out. He invites us to be the channels of His activity, not the substitute for it. Ishmael was Abraham's work. Isaac was God's work. Ishmael's birth could be explained by Abraham's scheming, planning, and working. Isaac's birth could only be explained by God's intervention and working. It is so fantastically liberating to face the demands that God makes and the promises that God makes and to realize that He alone is the means of their fulfillment. It is not that we just take a passive stance, as we shall see later, for although we are told to "work out your salvation in fear and trembling," it is on the basis of it being "God who works in you to will and to act according to his good pleasure" (Phil. 2:12–13).

Moses, at the age of forty, realized his destiny. A son of Hebrew slaves, he had been brought up in the Egyptian palace enjoying all the privileges of royalty since that memorable day when, as a baby hidden in the bulrushes to avoid the mass slaughter of Hebrew male babies, he had been found by Pharaoh's daughter and taken home as her own. At the age of forty, being aware of his true identity, the horrors of Hebrew slavery and that "God was using him to rescue them" (Acts 7:25), he dedicated himself to doing the will of God. His motivation was good, his sincerity genuine, but his actions disastrous. He wanted to fulfill what he knew to be the will of God and to liberate his people. So when he saw an Egyptian mistreating a Hebrew, beating him while he engaged in hard labor, he decided to act. Glancing to his left and to his right, thinking no one knew, he attacked the Egyptian, killed him, and buried him in the sand. But he was seen, and the news traveled fast. The reports reached Pharaoh, who, when he heard it, "tried to kill Moses" (Ex. 2:15). Moses fled, arrived in the desert of Midian, and stayed there for the next forty years. His dreams of liberating the Hebrew slaves lay shattered, yet he had been sure "God was using him to rescue them."

Moses, like Abraham before him, had offered to God only his dedication to do the work for God, leaving God Himself on the sidelines. He was eighty years of age before God would pick up the pieces of Moses' life and begin to do something with him. When

God met with him at the burning bush some forty years after he had fled from Egypt, it was a different Moses with whom He did business. Dead to his own ability and resources, for he had tried so gallantly and failed so miserably, his first question in response to God's call to go back and deliver His people was: "Who am I, that I should go to Pharaoh and bring the Israelites out of Egypt?" (Ex. 3:11). If only he had asked that same thing forty years before! Then it had been an attitude of "I am the man for the job." God's response to Moses' question was to ignore it, for "who am I?" is never the issue. He replied, "I will be with you" (v. 12) for that is the issue! The resources necessary for the task were not to be found in who Moses was, but in who God was! Moses responded by asking, in effect, "Who are you?" Have you ever taken time to ask God that question and then listened, really listened, to His answer? "God said to Moses, 'I am who I am. This is what you are to say to the Israelites; I AM has sent me to you'" (Ex. 3:14). God made Himself known as the Eternally Present One. Not a God who *was* at the burning bush giving the instructions. Not a God who *will be* at the final destination in the promised land. But a God who *is*, at all times operating in the present tense of life and to be counted on as being sufficient and available.

This is a fundamental principle of Christian living. God was not just active in the Cross, so that we only look back with gratitude for what He has done. He is not now waiting just to receive us into heaven. His purpose is to become active in the present tense of your experience, in every area of your life. Paul wrote, "The one who calls you is faithful and he will do it" (1 Thess. 5:24), for He calls us to a task not that we might do it for Him, but that we might become the means through which *He* does it! Moses learned the principle. The release of the children of Israel having been negotiated through the repeated intervention of God, they finally set off on the journey to the new land of Canaan. Everything was going well. After four hundred years of slavery the nation was enjoying a freedom and a dignity they had lost all consciousness of. The wind was behind them, new horizons of glory beckoned them, and God was in business on their behalf. But for many, the celebrations were short-lived. It wasn't very long before this marching nation of six hundred thousand men, plus women and children, were on the banks of the Red Sea. Moses had led them this far, but they couldn't cross over. It was too wide to bridge, too deep to wade, and too long to go around. Some of the people began to murmur and complain. Meanwhile they looked over their shoulders and there on the horizon behind them they saw a great cloud of dust, and in the dust the silhouette of the Egyptian army! Pharaoh had changed his mind, and having released them under pressure, he was now coming to round them up and take them back again to be his slaves. With a Red Sea in front which it was impossible to cross over and a sophisticated army behind which it was impossible to resist, the people were terrified. Was it a trick? Was Moses on the side of the Egyptians? Was it because there were no graves in Egypt that they were being brought here to die on the banks of the Red Sea? There was terror, panic, and confusion in the camp.

How was Moses to respond? How would you have responded in circumstances like this? "Moses answered the people,. 'Do not be afraid. Stand firm and you will see the deliverance the Lord will bring you today. . . . The Lord will fight for you; you need only to be still'" (Ex. 14:13–14). How could Moses speak like that? Surely it was irresponsible to respond to a situation that would at best return them to slavery, or at worst annihilate them, by just announcing "The Lord will fight for you." "Moses, stop just being spiritual about this," some may have thought. "You have got to do something. Be practical!" I suggest to you that Moses prayed and said something like this: "Lord, we have a big problem! We have the Red Sea in front, and we can't cross it. We have the Egyptian army behind, and we can't possibly defend ourselves against them. The people are in a state of panic, and I have no idea what we should do. But I want to remind You of something. It wasn't my idea to come here, it was Yours. You called me at the burning bush and I told you I wasn't able, but You said You would be with me. You also said we would go to Canaan, and as this isn't Canaan it is inconceivable that we would die here on the banks of the Red Sea, for You always mean what You say. So although I don't know how we are going to get out of this, You do. It is Your responsibility and I trust You. So, thank You. Amen."

Then, turning to the crowd Moses could say, "The Lord will fight for you," and under his breath he may well have added, "But please don't ask me how! Because I don't know." Do you see the difference in Moses now compared to when he was forty? Then, he dedicated himself to setting the people free. Now, he has died to his own techniques and scheming and is trusting the One who called him to do it. You will remember how God opened up the Red Sea and used the first problem to swallow the second problem, as the Egyptian army drowned in the sea while the Israelites went over on dry ground. God was in business now! God was winning the victories! God was active!

This is the essence of all Christian activity and life. This is what had been missing in my own understanding of what it meant to be a Christian during the first years of my experience. I did not understand the instruction to "Fix our eyes on Jesus, the author and perfector of our faith" (Heb. 12:2). I knew Christ was the "Author," for He had enabled me to become a Christian, but I did not know He was the "Perfector," or as other versions have it, the "Finisher" of our faith. Having allowed Him to begin, I thought it was my job to finish. I didn't know the verse which states, "He who began a good work in you will carry it on to completion until the day of Jesus Christ" (Phil. 1:6). Of course it was Christ who began the good work, but I was trying to complete it. I had not heard that it was, "just as you received Christ Jesus as Lord, continue to live in him" (Col. 2:6), and that my ability to continue to live in Him was on the same grounds as those upon which I received Him, that is, through an attitude of repentance and faith. In fact, the Bible is alive with verses and statements I had never been able to appreciate, which talk about Christ as the life and source of all true spiritual activity.

It is this that makes Christianity something far more than just another religion, far more than just some wishful thinking, and far more than a never-ending struggle to live a quality of life which in my more honest moments I recognize to be humanly impossible. It is not an escape from reality, but a plunge into reality where we begin to live life as God always intended it to be lived and discover the resources to be the men and women we were created to be.

However, this may be arriving at conclusions too quickly. The New Testament challenges its readers to "always be prepared to give an answer to everyone who asks you to give the reason for the hope that you have" (1 Peter 3:15). It is one thing to be able to give the hope and explain *what* is true, yet another to know the reason for the hope, and able to explain *why* it is true! To speak of God being actually present and working in our lives may be an exciting thing, but we need to understand *why* and *how* this is possible if we are to enter fully and intelligently into the good of it.

2

Good for Nothing

Before discussing the actual content of Christian experience, it is essential to consider its purpose. It is not enough to ask, "What is a Christian?" but "Why be a Christian?" Our understanding of *why* one should be a Christian will have considerable bearing on our ability to appreciate and enjoy the means to fulfilling that. Many resign themselves to a low-quality experience of God because they have never sought to find out clearly what God is actually wanting to do, and in consequence they do not expect very much to happen. Our experience will rarely exceed our expectancy, and when we expect little more than the forgiveness of our sins in the past and the prospect of heaven in the future, it is not surprising that the Christian life remains full of frustration in the meantime.

God's purpose for man has not changed. His reasons for creating man in the beginning remain His reasons for perpetuating man in the present. The first declared word by God about man recorded in the Bible is: "Let us make man in our image, in our likeness" (Gen. 1:26). This simple-sounding statement constitutes the ultimate role of man, from which he derives his dignity, his significance, and his right to be alive. The "image" and the "likeness" of God is not a physical one of course, for God is not a physical being. John writes, "No one has ever seen God" (John 1:18), and Jesus declared, "God is Spirit" (John 4:24). He does not have a body as we do, and any speaking of God in the Bible as having "ears," or an "arm," or of His "eye" are figurative expressions and not intended to be understood as God operating within the confines of a physical body. The image therefore is not physical, but it is moral. That is, in the moral attributes of man there was to be an expression of the moral attributes of God. Man's character, man's behavior patterns, man's ambitions were designed to portray God's character, God's behavior patterns, God's ambitions. Therefore, in the role for which he was created, were you to observe man in action—the way he went about his daily work, the way a husband and father would care for his family, the way a mother would bring up her children, the way employers would treat their employees and employees respect and work for their employers, the way people spent their money and their time, and the way they talked to their neighbors (and the way they talked *about* them)—you would see what God is like. The character of God in all its beauty, kindness, and tenderness would be visible in the lives and conduct of those created to be His image. Man, not just by what he says, but by what he *is*, was designed to be a revelation of God.

However, things have very clearly gone wrong! Were you and I to arrive on the earth today as complete strangers to this corner of the universe, knowing nothing about the earth other than the fact that God had placed here a creature called "man" who had been made in the image of God, we would receive a most unpleasant shock! Perhaps, being very keen to find out what God is like, we would set ourselves to observe man with great expectancy. If we could just see people in action for a while, visit their homes, walk their streets, and watch their television sets, we would legitimately expect that because they were made in God's image, we would discover what God is like. But as we carefully watched, we would grow increasingly horrified! If this is an expression of what God is like, we would rather have not known! God is greedy, we would conclude. He is often full of hatred, envy, and jealousy. He sometimes rapes, kills, steals, and fights. He is proud, often racially prejudiced, and His first concern seems to be always and only Himself. But why? Why such a distorted picture? Why is man, created for such dignity, so debauched? Why do his lifestyle and behavior patterns bear such a consistently false witness about God? Somewhere along the line, something, somehow has gone tragically wrong. If man's role was to express the likeness of God, his means of doing so have clearly been lost. This is true of you, and it is true of me. The essential ingredient that would make others aware of God when in our presence is missing.

ALIENATION FROM THE LIFE OF GOD

The missing ingredient is GOD HIMSELF. God did not create man to function and to fulfill his role in independence of Him, but to be inhabited by God, so that the very presence and life of God might be the enabling in man. The apostle Paul, diagnosing the present condition of men, describes them as being "darkened in their understanding and separated from the life of God" (Eph. 4:18). Earlier he had written to those who were now Christians: "As for you, you were dead in your transgressions and sins, in which you used to live" (Eph. 2:1–2). Although physically alive, he speaks of them as having been "dead," for it is spiritual life, which is nothing less than the life of God, that equips man to be what he was intended to be.

In the Garden of Eden, God had said to Adam: "You are free to eat of any tree in the garden; but you must not eat from the tree of the knowledge of good and evil, for when you eat of it you will surely die" (Gen. 2:16–17). He was not speaking only of physical death, but that in consequence of that act of disobedience, the life of God would be withdrawn from the experience of man, and while remaining physically alive he would be spiritually dead. This death is what Paul describes as "the wages of sin" (Rom. 6:23). Those wages were paid in the Garden of Eden when man chose disobedience rather than obedience, independence rather than dependence on God, and in consequence, "in Adam all die" (1 Cor. 15:22). The whole human race died in Adam, and all born since have been born in a state of being spiritually dead. It is not correct to speak of people today having to die *for* their sin, as some future event, because death *for* sin took place in Adam. However it is true to say that although we cannot die *for* sin, we can die *in* sin. That is, we can remain in our condition of alienation from God and suffer the eternal consequences. The only alternative to remaining dead is a very simple one. It is to come alive! This, as we shall see, is the Gospel invitation. It is an invitation to exchange death for life, and as a result, to exchange sin for righteousness.

CAPACITY AND CAPABILITY

Man's problem then, is that he has become alienated from the life of God, and while retaining the *capacity* for godliness he has lost the *capability* for godliness. His capacity for godliness is evidenced in his frustration with evil and his desire for good, but his lost capability is seen in his repeated failure to perform what he wills.

The apostle Paul talked honestly about the conflict between his *capacity* for godliness and his *capability* for godliness in his letter to the Romans. "I do not understand what I do. For what I want to do I do not do, but what I hate I do" (Rom. 7:15). There are things in life, he is saying, that I know are right and that I want to do. But I don't do them! There are things in life that I know are wrong, and I determine not to do them. But I do! What I want and what I do lie in conflict with each other. Herein lies the problem. My *capacity* for goodness, which deep down I believe in and long to fulfill, is frustrated by my *capability* for goodness, which lets me down again and again. Having been created in God's image and likeness, the possibility for that, the potential for that, the consciousness of that purpose remains latent in my being but seems so utterly detached from the power to accomplish it. The very capacity which motivates and inspires me to try to do and to be what is right, now condemns me by creating the consciousness of failure and guilt.

Some time ago, I spent a few days visiting a detention center in the southwest of England. I was leading a series of meetings in a nearby church and had been invited to spend part of my afternoons at the center throughout the week. I normally got there in time for a meal, and following that I would be given a group of about thirty boys, aged from fourteen to sixteen, with whom I would spend the next hour or so. The plan was that in the course of the week I would have the opportunity of speaking to all one hundred and fifty residents in the center. One afternoon we were having a constructive time talking about the things we wanted most out of life and how we hoped to accomplish them. I had written on a blackboard the things they had said would make life meaningful and happy, and we were in the process of discussing some of them when one of the boys interrupted with a very interesting comment. "My biggest problem is myself," he said, "and until I get this sorted out, nothing else is going to work." He went on to explain that he was in this same detention center for the third time, not because he enjoyed being there (and after graphically describing how and why he hated being there, he left us in no doubt that he meant it!), "but I am here," he went on, "because each time, I have found myself in a situation where I have been unable to resist doing something I knew was wrong, that deep, deep down I did not want to do, that I knew I would hate myself for doing, but which I went and did anyway. Until I can handle myself, I don't think much else is going to go right for me."

I asked the rest of the group how many of them would identify with that. How many of them would acknowledge that their biggest problem was themselves. It was the majority who agreed. I, too, know exactly what he was talking about, and so do you. The capacity and desire to do what is right is there. But the ability to do so is not. You may never have been sent to a detention center, but the problem is there and is real in your life. An electric light bulb that has been separated from its source of power retains the capacity to shine and give light, but it has become devoid of the capability and can no more produce the light it was supposed to transmit than a turnip could! This is the story of every human being living in separation from God. As Paul went on to state: "I have the desire to do what is good, but I cannot carry it out" (Rom. 7:18).

This is the nature of sin. The word *sin* means "to miss the mark." At one time the word was used in archery. As the archer took aim, shot his arrow toward a target and missed, it was called "sin." Whether he missed by half an inch, half a yard, or half a mile was irrelevant, for to have missed the target at all was sin. This is why the extent to which we have missed God's standard is secondary to the fact that we have missed at all, whether by little or by far. This is why James writes: "Whoever keeps the whole law and yet stumbles at just one point is guilty of breaking all of it" (James 2:10). If you miss a bus by one minute, one hour, or one day, the effect is the same. You have missed the bus! If you miss God's target by a little or a lot, the effect is the same. You have missed. Sin does not primarily measure how bad we are, it reveals how good we are not! We have missed the mark.

If sin is missing a mark, we are only in a position to recognize sin when we recognize the target we are designed to hit. Without a target we have nothing to hit and nothing to miss. Without knowing what we are to hit, we do not know when we have missed, which is why we cannot talk intelligently about sin without being aware of the target. Otherwise sin becomes only a vague notion, one person's opinion versus another person's opinion. The Bible describes the target: "For all have sinned and fall short of the glory of God" (Rom. 3:23). The target that sin is missing, the standard by which good is determined and by which bad is determined is the glory of God. Sin is only sin because it is inconsistent with the glory of God. Therefore we must ask, "What is the glory of God?" for it is only as we understand the target that we will understand sin.

THE GLORY OF GOD

The expression "glory of God" is used in the Bible with some slight variation of meaning. However, whatever its precise meaning in different contexts, it essentially speaks of the "nature and acts of God in self-manifestation. What He essentially is and does."[1] Therefore the target, the "glory of God," is the character of God. This immediately rings true, for it was that man would express the character of God that he was created in the first place. This is the image of God about which we have been thinking, and it is our failure to fulfill that purpose for which we were made that constitutes our sin. Goodness is not an arbitrary notion, so that each person has equal right to decide what is good and what is bad. Neither are good and bad determined by a consensus of society. Jesus declared what is good when a rich young man said to him, "'Good teacher . . . what must I do to inherit eternal life?' 'Why do you call me good?' Jesus answered. 'No one is good except God alone'" (Mark 10:17–18). Goodness is an absolute, and goodness is the character of God. Something is only good because it is consistent with what God is, and conversely, something is only bad because it conflicts with what God is. Because the target against which sin is measured is the glory of God, it is only as I discover how I can be what God created me to be that I can deal with sin. How then is the glory of God restored to human experience? We need to look at the perfect man.

THE PERFECT MAN

In contrast to the failure of mankind as a whole, it was the constant hitting of the target that made Jesus Christ the perfect Man that He was. John writes of Him, "The Word became flesh and lived for a while among us. We have seen his glory, the glory of the one and only Son, who came from the Father, full of grace and truth" (John 1:14). In the years in which he observed Jesus of Nazareth, John saw the glory that the rest of us have come short of. That does not mean that there was some bright shining light behind the head of Jesus (as some artists have portrayed), but that in the behavior patterns of Jesus was seen the character of God. As He worked in the carpenter's shop in Nazareth, as He played His part in the family of Joseph and Mary, as He kicked a ball around in the street with His friends, as He engaged in public ministry—crossing

---

1. W. E. Vine, *Expository Dictionary of New Testament Words*.

the road to speak to the outcasts of society that everyone else would rather pass by, touching lepers who had not been touched by anyone for years, laying His hands on the sick, rubbing shoulders with the immoral, the thieves, the treacherous whom the self-respecting religious people of the day were careful to avoid—there was portrayed accurately and consistently what God is like. What He did, what He said, and how He said it persistently revealed God. Thus John could also write, "None has ever seen God, but God the only Son, who is at the Father's side, has made him known" (John 1:18). God cannot be seen physically, but what God is in His moral character has been made known in the life of Jesus. The writer of the book of Hebrews says that God "has spoken to us by his Son" and then goes on to say, "The Son is the radiance of God's glory and the exact representation of his being" (Heb. 1:3). What God is, the Son radiated. What God does, the Son represented.

Quite apart from what the Lord Jesus Christ did on the cross and by His resurrection as the climax of His work on earth, for the thirty-three preceding years He revealed God and expressed the glory of God by what He was, by what He said, and by what He did. Therefore, if we want to find out what a real man is supposed to be, look at Jesus Christ, for in His life as a man He exhibited the glory of God, the very thing we have come short of. Although Jesus Christ was different from us as far as His *origin* was concerned, for He was coexistent, coequal, and coeternal with the Father, as far as His *operation* as a man was concerned, He chose to live as a real man, demonstrating nothing more than that which was intended to be true for all men. Jesus Christ lived a sinless life, not simply because He did not do the things that are wrong, but more because He consistently did the things that are right. This means that His life and behavior patterns were a constant revelation of God to those who were in His company and who cared to notice.

It is one thing to be aware of *how* Jesus Christ lived, but it is more important to realize *why* He lived as He lived. To be aware of how Christ lived may draw from me an admiration of Him, or even a worship of Him, but were I to attempt to practically relate that to how I live my life, it would only reinforce my frustration, my weakness, and my disillusionment. A person may be a good soccer player, and kicking a ball around with his friends he might be the envy of all of them. But were he to then have a game with a professional team, he would probably begin to realize he was not quite as good as he thought he was! Were he to play for his national team in the World Cup, he would begin to get very frustrated, would hardly see the ball, and would find the crowd booing him off the field! Why? Because the higher the standard against which he plays and against which his own skills are judged, the more aware he is made of his inability and failure. If we only know *how* Jesus Christ lived, we might, out of a deep admiration for Him and sincere dedication to Him, try our best to imitate Him. But it would and could only frustrate us. For the more we examine His perfect life and try our best to copy Him, the more we will become aware of our failure. At best we are left only to gaze in wonder, glad that such a Man lived and fulfilled the purpose of God, but with no hope nor help as to how to live our lives.

WHY JESUS LIVED AS HE DID

Let us take a close look at why Jesus Christ, as a Man, lived such a beautiful life. You may be surprised and you will certainly be encouraged by what we shall discover.

In the light of the wonderful quality to Jesus' life, we discover that He said some things about Himself that are astonishing. Regarding His *activity*, He said, "I tell you the truth, the Son can do nothing by himself; he can do only what he sees his Father doing, because whatever the Father does the Son also does" (John 5:19). Of all the wonderful works that characterized the ministry of Jesus, the miracles of healing, the feeding of the five thousand, the stilling of the storm, and the raising of the dead, He claimed to do nothing. He even went further than that to say, "The Son *can* do nothing by himself."

Regarding his *judgments,* He said, "By myself I can do nothing; I judge only as I hear, and my judgment is just, for I seek not to please myself but him who sent me" (John 5:30). The Lord Jesus was characterized by an amazing discernment. He saw what people were behind their masks and He often exposed them. He understood people and they felt understood by Him. His opinions were always right. But as the source of His judgments, He claimed to do nothing.

Regarding His *speaking,* He said, "When you have lifted up the Son of Man, then you will know who I am (literally: "you will know I AM," revealing His deity) and that I do nothing on my own but speak just what the Father has taught me" (John 8:28). When Jesus spoke, the people who listened were amazed! "No one ever spoke like this man," they would say. "He taught as one who had authority," Matthew records as being the response of the crowd who listened as He preached the Sermon on the Mount. Luke records that when He first preached in Nazareth, they "were amazed at the gracious words that came from his lips." The words of Jesus were fresh, they were profound, they were penetrating and always made their mark. Crowds flocked to hear Him speak. But of all the words that came from His lips, He claimed to do nothing. *Nothing* seems such an empty word. It sounds so discouraging, so anticlimatic, and yet remarkably it is an important word in the humanity of Jesus.

Paul, writing about the incarnation of Jesus, says of Him: "Who, being in very nature God, did not consider equality with God something to be grasped, but made himself *nothing*, taking the very nature of a servant, being made in human likeness" (Phil. 2:6–7). If what he became is described as "nothing," it should not be too surprising that what He claimed to do was "nothing." Taking these statements seriously, as we must, Jesus' claim to be a Man was that He was good for nothing! He became nothing and He did nothing.

Before we examine this further in the life of Jesus, let us pause for a moment. Do you ever feel you are good for nothing? Are you ever frustrated over your inability to live as you should? Do you ever feel like Simon Peter, who, after a night of fishing, called out to Jesus who was standing on the seashore, "We have toiled all night and have taken nothing" (Luke 5:5, AV)? A lot of hard work, a lot of effort, a lot of zeal but nothing! Perhaps the only thing that has stopped you admitting it is that you feel God is expecting you to accomplish something, and rather than admit defeat you are determined to try all the harder. Here is part of the good news of the Gospel. It is not the whole Gospel, but it is a vital part. If you are feeling good for nothing, you are in good company, extremely good company. You are in the company of the Lord Jesus Christ. As a Man He became nothing, and by His own human resources He accomplished nothing. Does it surprise you to have discovered you are capable of no more than He was as a Man? And does it encourage you to know that He chose to be no more capable than you? In case it does surprise you, remember that Jesus said to His disciples, "Apart from me you can do *nothing*" (John 15:5). Paul, when talking about the problem of not doing what he wanted to do and doing what he did not want to do, says of himself, "I know that *nothing* good lives in me" (Rom. 7:18). As far as goodness is concerned,

Paul acknowledged he was capable of nothing. One of the greatest moments in the life of a Christian is when he faces up honestly to his being "poor in spirit" (Matt. 5:3) and realizes he is not capable of being the person he was created to be or of doing the things he is supposed to do, when left only with his natural strength and resources.

But that is not the end of the story! If the statements of Jesus are true how do we account for the fact that He obviously accomplished an enormous amount? Try telling the many who were healed that He did nothing. Try explaining it to the thousands who ate the loaves and fishes miraculously multiplied on two separate occasions and of which there were thousands of eyewitnesses. Try explaining it to the families of those who were raised from the dead that this Jesus actually did nothing. What would they make of it? What about the many who were amazed at His teaching, or others who were offended by His teaching and who subsequently organized His death in retaliation? Tell them He said nothing Himself! Of course He said things! He shook the nation like no one else had done. His impact in history and on the world scene today, two thousand years later, has been greater than any other living being in the history of the world. His life divides history into B.C. and A.D. Of course He did things! No one in history has done as much as He.

Do Christians, of whom Jesus said, "apart from me you can do nothing," accomplish things? The answer is obvious. They do. History is full of men and women who accomplished great things for God. We know their names and we read their stories. But we need to know how it was possible. How did Jesus Christ, as a Man, live the life He lived and do the things He did? How were the miracles performed? How did He speak with such authority? How did He consistently express the glory of God? How are we to do the same?

Did you notice that in each verse where Jesus talked about doing nothing Himself, He talked about the Father. "The Son can do nothing by himself . . . whatever the Father does the Son also does" (John 5:19). "By myself I can do nothing . . . I seek not to please myself but him who sent me" (John 5:30). "I do nothing on my own but speak just what the Father has taught me" (John 8:28). In each statement He is saying it was the activity of the Father that made His work what it was. He explained this clearly later: "Don't you believe that I am in the Father, and that the Father is in me? The words I say to you are not just my own. Rather, it is the Father, living in me, who is doing his work" (John 14:10). The explanation for all that Jesus was and did was the Father "living in me, who is doing his work." Jesus fulfilled His role as a Man on the understanding that God's presence and activity was indispensable to being a true man.

Does an electric light bulb shine? The answer of course is yes. It exists for that purpose, and you purchase it for that purpose. It may come in various shapes and sizes and may be capable of different strengths of light. But although intended to give light, in actual fact the bulb itself can do nothing. Were you to purchase a bulb, place it on your table, and expect it to shine, you would be disappointed! The reason for this is that although created to give light, it was never intended to give light by itself, existing in independence. It is so constructed that only as it is connected to an electric current will it give light. There is not anything necessarily wrong with the bulb if you put it in the butter dish and find it doesn't shine. It just wasn't made that way! It is only as you do what was intended to be done with a light bulb, place it in a light socket and switch on the electricity supply, that it will shine.

Similarly, man has been created in such a way that his ability to be what a man is intended to be is the presence of God within him and the power of God released through him. Man is no more capable of functioning in independence of God than a light bulb is in independence of electricity. Of course man can get by in a way a light bulb can't, but his ultimate accomplishment is nothing. Hence the Lord Jesus Christ said to His disciples: "Apart from me you can do nothing." That is why, living as a Man, Jesus had to say: "The Son can do nothing by himself." As we are brought back into a relationship with God, where on the basis of His work accomplished on the Cross we are forgiven of our sin and become indwelt by the Spirit of God, we receive by His presence within us all that we need to be what human beings were intended to be. We become like bulbs connected to the electric current, and the purpose of our creation can be restored. Therefore, if apart from God we can do *nothing*, the presence and working of God makes *something* inevitable, "For nothing is impossible with God" (Luke 1:37).

NOTHING IS IMPOSSIBLE

To be indwelt by God, giving Him the freedom to be at work in us and through us, makes "nothing" an impossibility. Before, it was impossible to do anything, now it is impossible to do nothing! We are presented with two options. Outside of God, "nothing" is inevitable, but in a true and functioning relationship with God, "nothing" is impossible. Our lives inevitably accomplish nothing, or it becomes impossible to accomplish nothing.

It is wonderful to know that having been forgiven of our sin, being indwelt by God and giving Him the freedom to direct our lives, give us our orders, and empower us by His Spirit, we now spend our time knowing that nothing is impossible! God is doing something, our lives do have significance, and things are being accomplished that are of eternal value. If Jesus could say, "Apart from me you can do nothing," the apostle Paul later wrote, "I can do everything through him who gives me strength" (Phil. 4:13). By "everything" he does not mean he can jump over the moon, but that all God has planned and intends for him is possible in the strength of Jesus Christ. Outside of Christ, nothing is inevitable. At the end of time, we will stand before God with empty hands. In Christ, nothing is impossible. At the end of time we will stand full of gratitude for all that God has chosen to do. Are you living a life where nothing is inevitable, or are you enjoying the life where nothing is impossible?

This is the purpose of the Gospel. The forgiveness of sin (as we shall see later) is a wonderful thing, the prospect of eternity in heaven is a thrilling prospect, but in a real sense those issues are incidental to the purpose of salvation. Forgiveness is the source of salvation, and eternal life in heaven is the result of salvation, but it is the restored relationship with God that is its main content. "For God did not appoint us to suffer wrath but to receive salvation through our Lord Jesus Christ. He died for us so that, whether we are awake or asleep, we may live together with him." (1 Thess. 5:9–10). Whether we are physically alive or dead, it is in "living together with him" that salvation is being experienced. God did not create man in the beginning just to be clean, therefore forgiveness in itself does not restore us to God's purpose. God did not create man in order to populate heaven, therefore to be heading for heaven does not in itself restore us to God's purpose. Man was created to be in God's image, so that in his company there is a constant reminder of what God is like. We have fallen short of the glory of God, and it is the restoration of that glory that is the purpose of salvation and the mark of a true Christian. This is the work of Jesus Christ. Paul speaks of the Gospel as "Christ in you, the hope of glory" (Col. 1:27). That, despite the popular explanation, does not mean the hope of heaven! "Glory" is that which we have sinned and come short of, and it is the restored presence of Christ within a person that is one's hope of being able to hit the target and fulfill the purpose of one's existence and to be a revelation of the character of God.

This is not an immediate or instant event, but a growing process. In this life there will be a continuous growth into the likeness of the Lord Jesus Christ, and it will not be complete until we are in His presence forever. Paul wrote, "We, who with unveiled faces all reflect the Lord's glory, are being transformed into his likeness with ever-increasing glory, which comes from the Lord, who is the Spirit" (2 Cor. 3:18). Growth in the Christian life is a growth in godliness, in which our behavior patterns express a harmony and consistency with God. But how do we begin to live this way? What is involved in such a life where to accomplish nothing is now impossible? We will seek to discover this in the next chapters.

3

Living on God's Terms

I was once talking with a girl in her late teens, and in the course of conversation I asked her, "Are you a Christian?" It was during a young people's Christian conference, and I thought it a perfectly reasonable question to ask in its context. "Yes, I am," she replied, "but I am not your sort of Christian." I was a bit taken aback by this, so asked her, "What sort of Christian are you?" to which she responded, "It is very personal to me and I would rather not talk about it." I couldn't help but add, "I am not concerned as to whether you might be my kind of Christian, or whether you have a special kind all of your own. What I am really concerned about is whether you are God's kind of Christian."

Although the word *Christian* may have come to mean a multitude of things to a multitude of people, after all is said and done there is only one kind of Christianity that is valid, and that is God's kind! We do not have the freedom to pick and choose the aspects of God's revelation that are attractive and disregard or ignore the parts we do not like, still call it Christian and expect it to work, or regard it as authentic. We can only live the Christian life on God's terms. Anything else may make us religious but will leave us powerless.

If you would stretch your imagination, suppose I wanted to travel from London to New York by air, but after consulting a travel agent I become unhappy with the information given me. The cost is too great, and the weight allowance too small. However, I really do want what the airline is offering so I decide I will have it on my own terms. Imagine that I then go to London airport, write out a ticket myself on a piece of paper the same size as a genuine ticket, being careful to include all the detail you would find on the real thing. I then take my place in the line and with a warm smile on my face hand the ticket to the man at the check-in desk. He would probably look at it, look at me, look at it again, and then hand it back saying, "I am sorry, but you cannot travel with that." "Why not?" I protest. "It says 'London to New York,' it has the name of your airline on the top, it has the correct flight number and departure time written on it, and the correct price written on the bottom right hand side." "I am very sorry," he might say. "The information may be correct, but the ticket is not valid and you cannot travel." Imagine I then write across the back of the ticket in bright red felt pen that this particular airline is the greatest. The agent would probably smile, say, "Thank you—not many people say that. But you still cannot travel." Suppose I take the ticket back and this time I put it to music and sing it to him. Then I teach him some new songs: "Amazing plane, how sweet the sound, that carries a wretch like me. I once was walking, but now I'm flying, was at home but now I am free!" I then invite him to join in and we sing it as a round, I start off and he joins in halfway through and we really have a good sing-along. At the end of the song he will probably turn to me and say, "Thank you so much for coming and cheering me up. I haven't had such a good sing for quite a while. But I am sorry, you cannot travel. Here is your ticket, would you please now go away!"

Why would I not be eligible for travel? Is it because my ticket says the wrong things? No, it may say the right things. Is it because I express the wrong sentiments? No, they might be very impressed with my praise of the airline. Is it because I sing the wrong songs? No, they might like my songs and even ask to use them in their television commercials. There is only one reason why I cannot travel, and it is a very simple one. My ticket is issued by the wrong authority. The only ticket that is valid is the one issued by the airline in response to the right conditions being met, and anything short of that is invalid.

People can express all the right sentiments about Jesus Christ, sing the right songs, go to the right church, and use the right vocabulary, but unless they are living on God's terms, where He has issued the "ticket" and the right conditions have been met, they will have a Christianity that just won't work. They will discover that when they want to "fly," the ticket will bounce at the check-in desk. There will be no power in their lives, no consciousness of God, the Bible will remain dry, prayer will be a chore, and no one will ever see a living God being active in their lives.

The terms of Christian living are not up for debate or for

negotiation. I live the Christian life on God's terms, or I do not live it at all. Therefore our business is to find out God's conditions and be very careful to meet them.

THE COST OF FREE SALVATION

Let us face realistically that there is a cost to becoming and to being a Christian. We talk about salvation being "free," and this is wonderfully true but only in a limited sense. It is free in so far that we cannot purchase it or earn it, nor can we in any way bargain for salvation on the basis of our own goodness. "For it is by grace you have been saved, through faith—and this not from yourselves, it is the gift of God—not by works, so that no one can boast." (Eph. 2:8–9). In this regard, the Christian life is absolutely free, and were it to be anything other than that we would be without hope. Eternal life, states Paul, is "the gift of God" (Rom. 6:23).

However, in the ministry of Jesus Christ He never talked about salvation as free. He always talked about it as costly. Furthermore, He instructed people to count the cost and to respond on the basis of a willingness to pay that cost. For the Christian life to be free does not mean that it is cheap, that it is obtainable by little more than nodding one's head in God's direction, or by just believing a few facts about Him. There is a cost that must be met. "Large crowds were traveling with Jesus, and turning to them He said, 'If anyone comes to me and does not hate his father and mother, his wife and children, his brothers and sisters—yes, even his own life—he *cannot* be my disciple. And anyone who does not carry his cross and follow me *cannot* be my disciple. Suppose one of you wants to build a tower. Will he not first sit down and estimate the cost to see if he has enough money to complete it? For if he lays the foundation and is not able to finish it, everyone who sees it will ridicule him, saying, "This fellow began to build and was not able to finish." . . . In the same way, any of you who does not give up everything he has *cannot* be my disciple'" (Luke 14:25–33). Therefore we must take seriously the cost, we must understand it and count it, and only on the basis of paying the cost will we have the right to call ourselves "Christian" and be equipped to enjoy a relationship with God that will actually work.

A man came to Jesus on one occasion requesting eternal life, and the Lord Jesus refused him! He went away with nothing. His request was genuine, but he was not willing to pay the price. "As Jesus started on his way, a man ran up to him and fell on his knees before him. 'Good teacher,' he asked, 'what must I do to inherit eternal life?'" (Mark 10:17). That was a good question, and the way in which he asked it indicated an earnestness and genuineness that would have impressed you or me had we been present in the crowd. He came running. He fell on his knees oblivious to the embarrassment such a public gesture might have caused. He asked for the right thing. After a short discussion Jesus told him, "One thing you lack." There was just one issue that needed to be dealt with if he was to receive what he was requesting. The following words of Jesus probably surprised the crowds and shocked the man, "Go, sell everything you have and give it to the poor, and you will have treasure in heaven. Then come, follow me" (Mark 10:21). Like it or not, that was Jesus' very precise prescription for receiving eternal life! The man was not impressed. "At this the man's face fell. He went away sad, because he had great wealth" (Mark 10:22). Earlier Mark specifies that "Jesus looked at him and loved him" (v. 21), yet when the man chose to leave, Jesus allowed him to go. As far as we know, he never did receive eternal life. Jesus did not call the man back and say something like, "I am sorry I made it so hard for you. I didn't mean to frighten you away. Let's negotiate a relationship. What kind of Christian would you like to be? If you are not willing to sell everything, how much are you prepared to give away?" The terms of receiving eternal life were not open to discussion, negotiation, or compromise.

What is the issue here? Is it wrong to be rich? The simple answer to that is no. The Bible never says it is wrong to be rich. Jesus did say, "How hard it is for the rich to enter the kingdom of God" (Mark 10:23), and the Bible warns of the dangers of riches and of aspirations to them. "People who want to get rich fall into temptation and a trap and into many foolish and harmful desires that plunge men into ruin and destruction. For the love of money is a root of all kinds of evil. Some people, eager for money, have wandered from the faith and pierced themselves with many griefs" (1 Tim. 6:9–10). There is much warning in Scripture about the dangers of desiring wealth, but it is not the possession of wealth in itself that is wrong. Sometimes God even made people rich. The issue is a much more fundamental one, this man's riches being an expression of the real issue rather than the issue itself.

During His Sermon on the Mount, Jesus had said, "No one can

serve two masters. Either he will hate the one and love the other, or he will be devoted to the one and despise the other. You *cannot* serve both God and money" (Matt. 6:24). In His conversation with the man Jesus had diagnosed a god already evident in his life—his possessions. He was saying to the man in effect, "If you want to receive eternal life, you must understand that this will involve receiving a new master, a new Lord. Eternal life is not the receiving of a commodity, but the receiving of a person, the person of God Himself. And God, by virtue of who He is, does not come to occupy a position any less than that which will enable Him to be God and act as God." But the man had a problem. He already had a master, a god, a factor that motivated his activities, inspired his decisions, and determined his values. The god was his possessions, his money, his material goods, and as it is not possible to serve two masters, there would have to be a rejection of the present god before there could be a reception of the true God, whose presence in the man would be the gift of eternal life. Jesus was saying to him therefore, "In order to receive eternal life, you must sell your possessions, give to the poor, which means in other words, you must dethrone your god and then come and follow me." Tough stuff? It may sound so, but it deals with the basic issue of Christian living from which there is no compromise. The Lord did not negotiate a lower standard with him or make him an exception to the rule, but He sent him away lovingly, firmly, and with no confusion in the mind of the man. He had not received what he had asked for. He was not a Christian.

Before looking a little more at this man, let us pause for a moment. I wonder what would happen if a man such as this came into many of our churches today, ran to the front, fell on his knees, and asked, "What must I do to inherit eternal life?" What answer would he receive? How would YOU answer him? Taking the broad spectrum of Christendom, I fear that there might be a thousand different answers that might be given. Many formulas have emerged and evolved over the years, the process being in the direction of it becoming cheaper and easier. Some would tell him that he only needed to be baptized, join the church, and participate in its activities. In many churches I know, I fear we would sit him down and tell him, "It is all very simple. All you have to do is to ask Jesus to come into your life." That expression has evolved as popular evangelical terminology, although it is not to be found anywhere in the New Testament. No one in the Bible was ever told to ask Jesus into his or her life. But for many, this has not only become an accepted means of becoming a Christian, but has derived the status of orthodoxy and is regarded as the *only* means of becoming a Christian. It is perfectly true that Christ comes to live within a person, and this is in fact the act that makes a person a Christian as we shall see later, but to tell a person that Christ comes in just by asking is unwise, unbiblical, and misses the main issue. But this might be said to the man, and having prayed a prayer of acceptance of Christ we would ask, "Did you mean that?" If his reply was positive, we would assure him that he was now a Christian. We would probably give him a few tips on how to grow, read his Bible, pray, attend church, and then send him away. We would pass the word around the church that this rich young man had been converted. We would all get excited, especially the treasurer! It might well be arranged that in a few weeks' time we have a message on giving and capitalize on this new convert! Because he would have been a big fish to have landed, we would arrange for him to give his testimony (Luke, in his record of this encounter describes the man as a "ruler" as well as being "rich" and "young"), get him to speak at a few business luncheons, and use him to the fullest. The only problem would be that if you went to the church prayer meeting some six months later, you would find them praying for the rich young man. They would tell you, "He is backsliding. He is growing cold. He is losing interest." But he is not backsliding, he is not even a Christian. The tragedy would be that the next time someone tries to speak to him about Christ he would probably say, "No thank you. I have tried that once, and it doesn't work."

The man who came to Jesus went away with absolutely no confusion in his mind. He was not a Christian. He had not tried anything. He was still outside of Christ. He did not have eternal life. And he knew it!

RICH, YOUNG, AND RULING

Let us attempt to get under the skin of the rich young ruler and try to understand him. We know little about him except for three things. He was rich. He was young. He was a ruler. That is all we really know about him, which is why we call him the "rich young ruler"! When you stop to think about it, all three of these things are attractive. It is attractive to be rich. To be rich is a relative thing, and most of us have probably dreamed about being rich, by the standards of our own society. It is attractive to be young, especially when you are past forty! One of the nicest compliments you can pay people is to give them the impression they are younger than they really are. It is also attractive to be a ruler. The Bible does not reveal what it was he ruled, but whatever the sphere, part of his life was telling other people what to do and expecting them to do it. That must have been nice too! However, as he sat down and though, he probably realized an enormous problem. Although he enjoyed being rich, being young, and being a ruler, one day it would all have to end. One day he would die. When he died, he knew, he wouldn't be rich any more, as someone else would inherit his wealth. He wouldn't be young any more, and he wouldn't be a ruler any more. Someone else would have his authority delegated to him or her. He also knew he didn't have to be old to die, he could die while still young. He could have a camel crash the next day! "There is only one solution to my problem," he probably mused, "and that would be to have a life that would never end."

Someone may have said to him, "Have you ever heard of Jesus of Nazareth?" "No, who is He?" he would have responded. "He is a preacher." "What is He preaching about?" "Eternal life." "Eternal life? That is the very thing I need. If only I could be sure of eternal life, my basic fears and needs would be met. I will go and see Him." And he did. He ran, broke through the crowd, threw himself onto his knees, and said in effect, "I have a need, and you have the answer. What must I do to inherit eternal life?" The answer Jesus gave him sent him away as empty as he had come.

The Christian life begins with surrender to the lordship of Jesus Christ. His coming into the world, His death on the cross, and His resurrection from the dead were in order to establish a relationship with man in which the surrender of man and the lordship of Christ would be fundamental. "For this very reason, Christ died and returned to life so that he might *be the Lord* of both the dead and the living" (Rom. 14:9). Paul also wrote, "And he died for all, that those who live should no longer live for themselves but *for him* who died for them and was raised again" (2 Cor. 5:15). Do you see the basic problem with the rich young ruler? He wanted Christ as his servant, not as his master. He wanted Christ to meet his need, not to tell him what to do. There is no experience of God on those terms. If someone comes to Christ and says in effect, "I want to experience you as my

Christ as Master, not servant.

Savior, but I do not want you to be Lord of my life to tell me what to do and how to live," that person will receive from the Lord Jesus Christ precisely nothing. And if we were to establish somehow that someone could become a Christian on those terms, then Jesus will one day have to apologize to the rich young ruler. Yet, as I travel and preach in many parts of the world I am concerned that this assumption is clearly made in the thinking of many people. There is the idea that there are two kinds of Christian. There is the average Christian, who knows Christ as Savior, whose past sins have been forgiven and who will go to heaven when he or she dies. But there is also a superdeluxe version, the person who takes it all much farther and has Christ not just as Savior but as Lord. So much preaching exhorts those who have already taken Christ as Savior to move on and equally acknowledge Him as Lord. But His ability to save is a consequence of His role as Lord. The basic issue we must face and come to terms with is the role of Jesus Christ as Lord, and in consequence of that we will begin to experience His work as Savior.

What do we mean when we speak of the "lordship of Christ" in our lives? We are not talking about a relationship in which there are no tensions, everything is well, and we are approaching something akin to sinlessness! We are not even talking about being filled with the Holy Spirit, as though that is a synonym for knowing Christ as Lord. We are talking about *an understanding of Him* that leads to *an attitude toward Him.*

An Understanding of Him

We tend to speak in very subjective terms when talking of the lordship of Christ. We talk about "making" Christ Lord. However, the Bible speaks in objective terms. It speaks of the lordship of Christ as an objective truth that does not become true when I believe in Him and submit to Him, but remains untrue if I do not believe; rather, it is a fact that is established and is true, whether I believe or whether I don't, whether I submit or whether I don't. The apostle Peter concluded his explanation of the Gospel on the Day of Pentecost by stating, "Therefore, let all Israel be assured of this: God has made this Jesus, whom you crucified, both Lord and Christ" (Acts 2:36). He is Lord, stated Peter, not because *we* make Him Lord, but because *God* has made Him Lord. The result of Jesus' life, work, death, resurrection, and exaltation to the right hand of God is that

He has been made Lord, and therefore it is as Lord that we must come to terms with Him.

If you are a citizen of one of the United States of America, I would not ask you if you had made the governor of your state your personal governor! You see, whether you like it or not, that person has been made governor and his or her administration would be the authority in the state, whether you voted for and liked the person or not. The issue is not, have you made him or her your governor, because that is an objective and established fact. The only issue of concern now is are you prepared to submit to the authority of his or her administration, or not?

Just suppose you said you were not prepared to submit to the government. Would that make its laws invalid? Of course not. Imagine you were driving along a road and you passed a sign that read, "speed limit 30," but you decide you want to travel at fifty miles per hour. So, you keep your foot down and presently you notice in your rear view mirror a white car with a blue flashing light on top, traveling at sixty miles per hour and about to overtake you. The car pulls up in front of yours, the driver beckons you to stop, and two police officers get out of their car and walk toward you. "Do you realize how fast you were going?" one of them asks. "Yes, at fifty miles an hour," you reply. "But do you realize you are in a thirty mile per hour speed zone?" he says, with one hand already holding his notebook and the other searching for his pen. "Yes I do," you respond, "but I want to ask you a question. Who decided that I should not exceed thirty miles per hour on this kind of road?" "It is government legislation," he would say, "passed as law by the government of this state." "Then it does not apply to me," you reply. "I did not vote for this administration, I do not like it, nor do I agree with it." Would that mean you were exempt? Of course not! The law of the land stands whether you agree with it or not. So, despite your protests you would be duly fined, and should you refuse to pay, you would go to jail. The government of your state and the law it imposes is an objective reality, and the issue you have to come to terms with is not whether you voted for it or agree with it, but whether or not you are prepared to submit to its authority.

Similarly the lordship of Christ must be understood as an objective reality. He is not Lord because we make Him Lord, but because God has made Him Lord, and whether I personally like it or not, all of history is going to wind up at the feet of Jesus Christ and will be answerable to Him. Paul stated, "God exalted him to the highest place and gave him the name that is above every name, that at the name of Jesus every knee should bow, in heaven and on earth and under the earth, and every tongue confess that Jesus Christ is Lord, to the glory of God the Father" (Phil. 2:9–10). The Bible teaches that the lordship of Christ is an established fact to the extent that in the course of time every person who ever lived will come to recognize this. This is why the Gospel is important. We do not preach the Gospel just because it works, but because it is true. A person needs to become a Christian not because of the needs in his or her life, but because Jesus Christ is true, and He is Lord. If we only preach the Gospel because it works, we compete with a thousand other things that may claim to work. If we preach Christ only because He meets needs, we have nothing to say to people whose lives are relatively trouble free and who feel able to handle the problems themselves. The Gospel is important because it is true. All of history has at some time to come to terms with the lordship of Jesus Christ, and the invitation is to do it now, freely and voluntarily, rather than to wait until the day when there will be no choices.

The issue is not one of making Christ Lord, but of submitting to Him as Lord. We may refuse to submit to the authority of the government, but we are still subject to its authority because it exists as a reality. We may refuse to submit to the authority of Jesus Christ, but we are still subject to Him along with the whole of mankind, and one day, to our acute embarrassment, we will discover that to be so. We have one basic choice with Jesus Christ, either to submit to Him voluntarily and freely, or to submit to Him under compulsion when "every knee shall bow . . . and every tongue confess that Jesus Christ is Lord." But if we wait until then, it will be the last thing we ever do! The act of becoming a Christian involves the voluntary act of surrender to Him now, His Lordship

AN ATTITUDE TOWARD HIM

On the basis of the facts that must be recognized about Christ, we have to adopt a right attitude toward Him. This was the issue with which the rich young ruler was confronted. Recognizing Him to be who He is—LORD, our response must be such that He is free to be what He is—LORD. We must acknowledge His exclusive right of government over our lives and set ourselves apart to Him with the desire that His purposes, His plans, and His pleasure might be our concern.

Before I married, there were, I imagine, a number of women I could have possibly married. There are in excess of two billion women in the world, and bearing in mind many were already married, some were too old and some were too young, let's take the round figure of 0.1 percent of the world's women that I could just possibly have married (that is, one possibility in a thousand). That would give me about two million possibilities. Quite a choice! However, the day came when, having fallen in love with a girl called Hilary, I asked her to marry me. She, amazingly, agreed, and when we married I made a commitment to "forsake all others, and keep myself only unto her as long as we both shall live." Having found this one out of the two million possibilities, suddenly the other one million, nine hundred, and ninety-nine thousand, nine hundred, and ninety-nine other possibilities became strictly unavailable to me and I to them. I surrendered the right to any other relationship of this nature, and Hilary became the exclusive object of my love and commitment as a husband.

This is a picture of the kind of relationship into which we must come with Christ. He is to be given exclusive rights as the authority in our lives, to the exclusion of everything else, even legitimate and good things. This is why Jesus made the statement, "If anyone comes to me and does not hate his father and mother, his wife and children, his brothers and sisters—yes even his own life—he cannot be my disciple" (Luke 14:26). This is not to say there is anything wrong in having a father, mother, wife, children, brothers, or sisters. Of course not! These relationships are good, right and should be some of the best on earth. But Christ takes priority over the things that are right and good as well as over things that are bad,

The day I married Hilary I was not making a statement about the good or bad in the other women of the world that I was not marrying. I was acknowledging that she would now hold a place in my life that would be beyond any other human relationship that I might have. However, the exclusive nature of marriage does not mean there are never going to be tensions, misunderstandings, or struggles. In a relationship as close as marriage these are inevitable, and there will be times when it is necessary to apologize and to deal with barriers that can grow between husband and wife. But the commitment remains, and the relationship is still the same. Similarly, in our relationship with Jesus Christ, our surrender to Him means that He is given a place of priority that is shared by no one else, but this does not mean that there will be no problems, no struggles, no sin, or no failure on our part. These will be inevitable. John wrote to Christians and stated, "If we claim to be without sin, we deceive ourselves and the truth is not in us" (1 John 1:8). But when we sin, we confess and turn from it, and He forgives. Despite the failings the relationship remains intact, and when all is said and done, our chief goal in life is to please Him and to serve Him.

I have often been asked the question, "How much do I have to give up to become a Christian?" I used to answer that by saying something like, "Well, it all depends . . ." and would then be as careful as I could so as not to frighten the inquirer and to indicate it was only the things that were bad for us anyway that we had to give up. I do not say that any more. In answer to the question I reply, "Everything." Jesus said, "Any of you who does not give up *everything he has* cannot be my disciple" (Luke 14:33). That does not mean that Jesus will take everything away, but that everything I have will now function under His authority and be conducive to His purposes. Apart from that, I *cannot* be a disciple. Do not, as I have sometimes heard done, distinguish between being a Christian and being a disciple with the idea that discipleship is on a deeper level. The word *Christian* began only as a nickname for disciples. "The disciples were first called Christians at Antioch" (Acts 11:26). It is as a disciple that one earns the right to be called a Christian, and therefore if I am not a disciple, fulfilling the demands of discipleship, I am not a Christian.

Does all this sound tough? Does it all sound one-sided, with me giving Christ everything? "What does His role as Lord mean to me?" you may be asking. We will think about that now, but all the many exciting benefits of His lordship in our lives are possible only as we come to terms with the cost, and as we are willing to pay it.

4

The Lordship of Jesus Christ

Some years ago, I remember going with a friend to a coffee house to talk about Jesus Christ to some of the young people who used to congregate there. It was in the days when coffee houses were popular meeting places for young people. I had only recently begun to talk openly about Christ to people, but my friend was much more experienced and I was glad to leave most of the talking to him. At one stage we were in conversation with a lad of sixteen or seventeen who showed a really open attitude to what we were saying. My friend was very carefully and kindly showing him that the true meaning and purpose for our existence could be found in Christ. After they talked for what could have been a couple of hours, the boy seemed to be at the point where he might be prepared to give himself to Christ. My friend, no doubt sensing the same thing, suddenly asked him a question, "In the light of all we have talked about this evening, can you think of any reason why you should not become a Christian tonight?" The young man sat for a few moments, then looking back at him replied, "No, I cannot think of any reason."

I was excited by this but to my amazement, my friend leaned across the table and said, "Then let me give you some!" For the next few minutes he began to explain something of the cost of being a Christian. He talked about the need to surrender his whole life, his future, his ambitions, his relationships, his possessions, and everything he was to God. Only if he was prepared to do this, my friend explained, could Christ begin to work effectively in his life.

Sitting opposite, I watched him sink back into his seat as he listened to what was being said, and I, in embarrassment, sank back into mine! My friend then seemed to lean even further across the table and asked, "Can you still not think of any reason why you shouldn't become a Christian tonight?" After another moment, the reply came, "I can think of some now," to which my friend responded, "In that case, do not become a Christian until you have dealt with every one of those reasons and are willing to surrender everything to Christ." Later, we exchanged addresses and arranged to meet him again.

When we got out onto the street, I was so angry with my friend. "What on earth were you trying to do?" I exploded. "That fellow was so close, and you went and frightened him away like that." To my surprise, he asked me, "What did Jesus do in circumstances like this?" I had never really thought about it, much less done a Bible study on it, but I gave him what seemed the obvious answer. "He invited people to follow Him as soon as possible." "You are wrong," he replied and proceeded to tell me that Jesus never made it easy for people to follow Him, spelling out the cost and the demands of discipleship to any who showed interest.

That night, we sat down together and studied the Bible to see how Jesus responded to those who wanted to follow Him. I was amazed! We looked at the rich young ruler who went away as empty-handed as he had come to Jesus. We looked at the man who came enthusiastically to Jesus and announced he would follow Him. Jesus replied, "Foxes have holes and birds of the air have their nests, but the Son of Man has no place to lay his head" (Matt. 8:19–20), and invited him to share in His homelessness. Another wanted to wait until his father died so that he could tidy up his affairs and then follow Him, but Jesus told him, "Follow me, and let the dead bury their own dead" (Matt. 8:22). After Jesus had spoken what some described as "hard teaching," John records, "From this time many of his disciples turned back and no longer followed him" (John 6:66). Jesus did not call them back but rather turned to the Twelve, who had stayed, and said, "You do not want to leave too, do you?" (John 6:67). Jesus, I began to understand, was not under a pressure to get results from His ministry but to communicate truth and discharge the responsibility given to Him by His Father irrespective of whether or how people responded. He loved people more than He loved results. He loved people enough to be honest with them. I realized I was more in love with statistics than with people. I would rather have gone home and told people that one person had come to Christ than be concerned that someone was doing real business with God.

One of the interesting features of Jesus' ministry was that from a statistical point of view, it did not look very effective! Were Jesus an evangelist in the twentieth century, the results of His evangelism would probably not be written up in the Christian press. And it was not that He didn't have many opportunities or speak to many people. On one occasion He spoke to five thousand men, plus women and children, and He fed them miraculously with just five loaves of bread and two small fish. On another occasion He fed four thousand men, plus women and children, this time with seven loaves and a few fish. Wherever He went great crowds would flock to hear Him preach and to witness the miracles He performed. The diseased and dying were brought to Him, and He healed "all the sick" (Matt. 8:16). From Galilee to Jerusalem people knew about Him, discussed and debated about Him, and either loved Him or hated Him. When He rode into Jerusalem just a few days before His death, He was greeted by many who spread their cloaks on the road while others spread branches they had cut and brought from their own fields, and they all shouted out to Him, "Hosanna! . . . Hosanna in the highest!" (Mark 11:9–10). Yet, despite all the acclaim and the many who were healed, despite the crowds who listened to His teaching and those who witnessed His miracles, there were very few who became His disciples. It is impossible to know how many there were, but soon after His death and prior to His ascension there gathered together in Jerusalem no more than one hundred and twenty to wait for the coming of the Holy Spirit at Pentecost. A total of one hundred and twenty disciples after three years of public ministry is an average of less than one per week! Not the kind of story that makes news in the Christian press.

Why did so few follow and stick with Jesus? Even His crucifixion was put to a popular vote, and by an overwhelming majority, He was sentenced to death. Pilate, being too weak to make the decision himself, offered the crowds the option of having Jesus or a notorious robber and murderer named Barabbas released. Pilate, I believe, was shocked by the result. With this choice it was inconceivable the crowd would ask for the release of Barabbas. He was a man many of the people feared. They kept their doors locked when he was around. The children would be kept off the streets and women would not be allowed out on their own when Barabbas was in town. He was a wicked man. Justice would be done, many probably thought, the day Barabbas hangs on a Roman cross. Pilate gave them the option of having Barabbas back on their streets as a free and pardoned man, if they wished.

Or they could have Jesus back on the streets. No one ever needed to lock their doors to keep Him away. No one shielded their children when He was around, for He loved them and they loved Him. They would welcome Jesus into their homes. They would pour out their needs to Him and He would understand. They would bring their sick to visit Him. He touched people no one else had touched for years. He crossed the road to meet with the outcasts of society and ate meals in the homes of notorious sinners. The self-righteous people hated Him, but the common people loved Him.

Pilate got a shock when he offered the crowd the choice of Barabbas or Jesus. They called for Barabbas! "But what shall I do with this man Jesus?" called Pilate. "Crucify Him," they thundered back, "Crucify Him."

Why was there such a response to Jesus? He explained it in a parable He told just before He went to Jerusalem for the last time. The reaction was simple. "We don't want this man to be our king" (Luke 19:14). In the emphatic wording of the Authorized Version, "We will not have this man to reign over us." It is the demands of kingship that divide. People will come to Christ for what they can get from Him, but when He demands their allegiance they will turn their backs. Jesus had few converts but many enemies at the end of His ministry, because the rock-bottom issue the people eventually had to face was His kingship. You have to face that issue. And so do I. Not just once, but continually.

WHY ARE WE AFRAID OF GOD?

Why are so many fearful of the lordship of Christ in their lives? I have talked to many who want to be right with God but who are frightened of surrendering to Him. I remember seeing an eighteen-year-old girl in tears, after a meeting at which I had spoken in her school in South Wales, when she told me how she wanted to give herself fully to God but was scared of what He might ask of her. Scared He might call her to a job she didn't like, scared He might call her to marry a man she didn't love! These are the things that give concern to many people. If God has plans, there is the underlying fear they will not be good plans. If He has an occupation for someone to follow, it will be something he or she doesn't want to do—like being a dentist! (I do not understand why anyone would want to be a dentist!) If He has planned whom we should marry, one is afraid of what that person will be like. We will not be able to marry for love, but out of sheer, cold obedience. The basic idea is that if it is something someone doesn't like, God probably will, and if it is something someone does like, God probably won't! I understand those fears for I have shared them.

I remember asking a class of pupils aged around thirteen or fourteen to tell me what they thought life would be like if they did only what God wanted from the time they got up in the morning until the time they went to bed at night from that day on until the end of their lives. The responses were interesting, but were all negative, with a major stress on how dull, boring, and dreadful life would be. The only positive comment came from one boy who said, "At least we wouldn't do anything that was wrong," to which someone else added, "But then we wouldn't have any fun!" I then asked them, "Where on earth do you get that idea of God from?" They actually replied, "From Christians." I discovered they didn't really know what a Christian was, and their impressions had been formed by the typical television image of weak, effeminate men, some of whom were called "Father" but dressed up like mother, something very, very different from the real thing! Many people have a terrible image of God in their minds, and although this incident took place with a group of non-Christian young people, many who would claim to be Christians have similar fears about doing what God wants them to do.

Whenever we have fears about God's plan, it is always for the same very simple reason. We do not know God well enough! Most of our negative fears about God derive from the fact we do not know God as He really is. As I write this I have a very young child who will evidence insecurity in the presence of certain people, and it is always for the same reason. She doesn't know them well enough. There is only one solution, and that is to give her time to get to know the person. I believe that many of the difficulties we face in Christian experience derive from not knowing God well enough. This is certainly true in my own life, and it is true for many others. Listen to the apostle Paul, "I know whom I have believed, and am convinced that he is able to guard what I have entrusted to him for that day" (2 Tim. 1:12). Paul says he is convinced of two things: (1) he knows whom he has believed, and (2) he knows the One whom he believes is able to guard what has been entrusted to Him. His conviction about the second thing is based on the first. It is knowing *whom* we believe that causes us to trust Him.

Notice Paul does not say, "I know *what* I have believed," but "I know *whom* I have believed," and there is all the difference in the world between the two. I enjoy being married, not because I have read some good books on marriage and could give a lecture or two on the subject, but because I know my wife and she is great to live with. The Christian life is more than knowing truths, it is knowing God. And the depth and reality of our experience is related directly to how well we know Him. In fact, every facet of the Christian life grows out of a knowledge of God. Jesus defined eternal life in this way, "Now this is eternal life: that they may know you, the only true God, and Jesus Christ, whom you have sent" (John 17:3). Eternal life is not a substance, it is a Person, and it is enjoyed by knowing the Person. It is knowing God and knowing Christ.

It is out of knowing *whom* we believe that Paul makes the second statement, "[I] am convinced that he is able to guard what I have entrusted to him for that day." There are no fears about those things Paul has entrusted to Jesus Christ, for "he is able to guard" them. If I had a thousand dollars of spare cash, I could either deposit it in a bank, or I could look after it myself. If I paid it into a bank account, it would become the responsibility of the bank to look after it and guard my money. I could relax about its security for I am convinced that the bank is able to guard what I have entrusted to it. What I am prepared to entrust to the bank, they are prepared to look after.

However, if I do not pay the money into the bank and decide instead to keep it at home under the mattress, I have to look after it myself. The bank will take no responsibility if some of it is missing, for I have not entrusted them with that responsibility. They undertake to look after what I entrust to them, but what I do not commit to them I have to look after myself.

What I commit to Jesus Christ and place in His hands, He undertakes to look after. What I do not entrust to Him, I have to look after myself. That is the simple choice we have to make. If I am afraid of Christ looking after the affairs of my life, it can only be because I either do not know Him well enough, or I do not want Him.

GOD'S PLANS ARE GOOD

God's plans may not always make us glad, but they are good! His plans may not always seem pleasant, but they are perfect! Paul describes the will of God as being "his good, pleasing and perfect will" (Rom. 12:2). When we see it to be good and we acknowledge it to be perfect, we will discover it to be pleasing. Sometimes the plans of God have taken His people through pain and suffering as they have allowed themselves to be the means of His will being accomplished. The Lord Jesus Himself went through agony as He ruthlessly carried out the will of His Father with no regard for His own comfort. In the Garden of Gethsemane, shortly before His crucifixion, He said to His disciples, "My soul is overwhelmed with sorrow to the point of death" (Matt. 26:38) and then He prayed, "My Father, if it is possible, may this cup be taken from me. Yet not as I will, but as you will" (v. 39). We must be honest and we must be realistic. There is a price to pay for obedience. It takes us to the front line of the battle with Satan and his cohorts, and we are not exempt from danger, tears, or pain. But through it, beyond the immediate suffering, beyond the unanswered questions, beyond the pain of battle, there is good that God is accomplishing, and it is perfect, and when we see the whole picture, there will be no doubt that it is pleasing. Isaiah, seeing down the corridor of time, anticipated in some detail the sufferings of the Lord Jesus, and he wrote, "It was the Lord's will to crush him and cause him to suffer . . . after the suffering of his soul, he will see the light of life and be satisfied" (Isa. 53:10–11). Beyond the agony of the cross the Lord Jesus saw the purpose and was satisfied.

God is under no obligation to explain to you or to me what He is accomplishing with our lives. Sometimes He will give a glimpse as He often did to people in Scripture, but otherwise there will be no explanations from heaven and we will "live by faith, not by sight" (2 Cor. 5:7).

A man in the Bible for whom much seemed to go wrong was Joseph. He had two disadvantages in life. He was the eleventh of twelve sons, and he was his father's favorite child. The second was a bigger disadvantage than the first, and his brothers hated him for it. In a dream one night, God gave Joseph a glimpse into his future when he dreamed he was out in the fields with his brothers, binding sheaves of grain; suddenly Joseph's sheaf stood upright and the rest of the sheaves bowed down before his. Later he had another dream in which the same thing was reaffirmed. This time the sun, the moon, and eleven stars bowed down before him. Joseph told his brothers of this, the implication being that they would all bow down to him one day. They, needless to say, hated him all the more for

this and decided to get rid of him. They arranged for him to go out
to the sheep one day, and while there they sold him to some passing
Midianite slave traders, who had him auctioned on the slave market
in Egypt. Meanwhile they took his coat of many colors, made for
him by his father, Jacob, and after dipping it in the blood of a goat,
took it home to provide evidence to convince Jacob that Joseph had
been killed by a wild animal. Jacob was heartbroken, and in his
sorrow his sons even managed to weep with him, despite the fact
that the twenty pieces of silver they had received for Joseph were
still jingling in their pockets.

Meanwhile in Egypt, Joseph was sold to the highest bidder, a
man named Potiphar, who was the captain of Pharaoh's guard.
Joseph was seventeen years old at this time and already there was
evidence he was a man "in whom is the Spirit of God" (Gen.
41:38). Whatever Joseph did, God caused him to prosper. Potiphar
was impressed and put Joseph in charge of his household. But
Potiphar's wife was impressed with Joseph too, but for different
reasons. She tried to seduce him, and one day when he was alone in
the house, she grabbed hold of him and invited him to bed with her,
but he fled from the house leaving his cloak in her hand. When
Potiphar came home she falsely accused Joseph of attempting to
rape her, and Potiphar in his anger had him thrown into prison. He
stayed in prison for many years. At the age of thirty, thirteen years
after being sold by his brothers, he was called before Pharaoh to see
if he could interpret a vivid dream Pharoah had had and which no
one else had been able to understand. Joseph told him, "I cannot do
it . . . but God will give Pharaoh the answer he desires" (Gen.
41:16). God gave the interpretation to Joseph, and he predicted to
Pharaoh that there would be seven years of plenty to be followed by
seven years of famine, and that during the years of plenty they must
prepare for the years of famine. As a result, Joseph was made
second to Pharaoh in the whole nation. During the next seven years
Joseph prepared for the years of famine to follow. The famine was
widespread and when Jacob, far off in Canaan, heard that there was
food stored in Egypt, he sent his sons to purchase some. On arrival
they were brought before Joseph. He was now a man of thirty-nine
years, having been sold by his brothers some twenty-two years
before. Joseph eventually made himself known to them as their
brother, but added, "Do not be distressed and do not be angry with
yourselves for selling me here, because it was to save lives that God

sent me ahead of you. . . . It was not you who sent me here, but God" (Gen. 45:5–8). Later, when his brothers feared Joseph might take vengeance on them for the way they had treated him all those years before, he explained, "You intended to harm me, but God intended it for good" (Gen. 50:20). Behind the seeming disaster in his life he saw the hand of God, and even more, he saw the goodness of God.

Had someone gone to Joseph in his prison cell and told him how wonderful it was that "in all things God works for the good of those who love him" (Rom. 8:28), he might have looked at that person strangely. As far as he could see, nothing had gone right! His best years were being spent either as someone else's slave or as a prisoner for a crime he had not committed. Meanwhile, back at home his father had never got over his broken heart after hearing of Joseph's death. "Do you call his sorrow good?" Joseph might well have asked. At that time he didn't know the whole story, but when he later began to see it, he could say "God intended it for good."

God is under no obligation to explain anything He does with us. Sometimes there will be no explanation at all in this life. Job, who suffered as much as anyone in the Old Testament, had no idea of what God was allowing to take place in his experience, and although he said he could not see God anywhere at the time, he was able to affirm, "He knows the way that I take; when he has tested me, I shall come forth as gold" (Job 23:10), and he stated at the beginning of his kaleidoscope of troubles, "Shall we accept good from God, and not trouble?" (Job 2:10). God's ultimate work is good, and its ultimate effect is good.

What is described as being "good" is not necessarily good for me. We have to see God's working on a wider canvas than that which has to do with our own comfort and good. What God does with me personally may be for the good of someone else and primarily for the good of God. That of course is good for us too, when we begin to live for the benefit of God and others as a primary concern.

I want to be realistic. To be surrendered to God does not mean everything is going to be comfortable. A Christian is not exempt from difficulties. If anything, he is equipped for them. He is able to go through life knowing that nothing touches him without the permission of God, and that he is in business not to be comfortable and cozy but to be effective and significant in God's overall purposes.

The hardships, the difficulties, and the tears are not the end of the story, for God is working out something good, something perfect, and something pleasing.

I suppose that one of the frequent questions I am asked, by young Christians in particular, is, "How do I know the will of God?" If we are concerned to be surrendered to the will of God, He doesn't always seem to cooperate by letting us know clearly what His will is! Is that how you feel sometimes? You ask for guidance and direction but appear to receive little. However, if God's greatest desire for you is that you fulfill His will, and your greatest desire is to do His will, there shouldn't be any difficulty. If there is a difficulty, somewhere along the line you have created it.

The specific will of God for us will only be found within the general will of God for all His people. There are four things the New Testament states as being God's will for you and me, and it will be within obedience to these specific instructions that His will for us individually will be found.

1. *That we be holy*: "It is God's will that you should be holy; that you should avoid sexual immorality; that each of you should learn to control his own body in a way that is holy and honorable" (1 Thess. 4:3–4). One criterion for fulfilling the will of God is a body that is sexually clean. Where there has been abuse and sin in that area in the past, it needs to be forgiven and cleansed. It is interesting to see how many occasions of sin in the Bible were the result of physical appetites that were out of control. The appetite for food is as big, if not a bigger, cause of sin than sexual appetite. Many people, from Eve in the Garden of Eden onward, ran into trouble over food. It was the first temptation the Devil brought to Jesus too, when He was alone in the wilderness. A holy body is necessary for the will of God. Paul called upon the Romans to "offer your bodies as living sacrifices . . . *then* you will be able to test and approve what God's will is" (Rom. 12:1–2). The relationship between a holy body and enjoyment of the will of God is a very clear one. Joseph proved that too.

2. *That we be thankful*: "Give thanks in all circumstances, for this is God's will for you in Christ Jesus" (1 Thess. 5:18). This verse does not say that we should give thanks *for* all circumstances but *in* all circumstances. We must see beyond the difficult

circumstances to the sufficiency and the sovereignty of God. God is always bigger than the problems, and His will for us is that we never cease to recognize that, being constantly thankful to Him for all that He is and for all that He is doing.

3. *That we are good*: "Submit yourselves for the Lord's sake to every authority instituted amongst men. . . . For it is God's will that by doing good you should silence the ignorant talk of foolish men" (1 Peter 2:13–15). By doing good, even in the face of injustice and foolishness, we are fulfilling the will of God. Joseph again proved this. In Potiphar's house, Joseph worked hard. "When his master saw that the Lord was with him and that the Lord gave him success in everything he did . . . Potiphar put him in charge of his household, and he entrusted to his care everything he owned" (Gen. 39:3–4). Later in prison, although there for wholly unjust reasons, he demonstrated a goodness and a godliness such that the prison warden "put Joseph in charge of all those held in the prison" (Gen. 39:22). If we are not prepared to live good lives where it is costly to do so, we are stepping out of the will of God.

4. *That we suffer*: "Those who suffer according to God's will should commit themselves to their faithful Creator and continue to do good" (1 Peter 4:19). It is not the will of God to alleviate every suffering, for there are times when the will of God is for us to suffer. This will vary from person to person, but when we find ourselves suffering, the will of God is not that we begrudge it, but commit ourselves to our Creator.

These four statements are the specific things the New Testament says about the will of God for us. These apply to all of us, and there are no exceptions. To discover the particular will of God for our lives we must be living within the general framework of His will. We must be holy people. We must be thankful people. We must be good people. We must be prepared to suffer willingly. It is within this framework that we discover the particular will of God for our lives, and also it is within this framework that our responsibility for finding the will of God ceases. Let me explain. We are never told in Scripture to ask God to show us His will for our personal lives. Have you ever noticed that? The will of God is a promise to us, and our task is to fulfill the conditions that enable God to fulfill His promise.

Solomon wrote, "In all your ways acknowledge him, and he will direct your paths" (Prov. 3:6). We are not told to pray for guidance but to acknowledge Him, and in response He will direct our paths. Directing our paths is God's responsibility, and it is as much His responsibility as getting us to heaven is. What is more, in the process of guiding us, God is under no obligation to explain what He is doing. God did give Joseph some idea when he dreamed about his brothers' sheaves bowing down to him, and no doubt in the prison years he often thought about that and knew he was destined for something more significant than being a convict all his life. When God gives you a vision of His purpose for your life, it is that you might still believe it when the going is tough and it all seems impossible. God wanted Joseph in the palace in Egypt, and the only way there was through the back door—in fact, through the dungeon door, and it would take thirteen years of captivity to bring it about. In contrast to Joseph, God gave no dream to Job to enable him to see beyond the years of awful suffering. God may tell you and me some things, or He may not. He is under no obligation. But as we awake each morning, we can turn to the Lord Jesus Christ with thankful anticipation that this day is in His hands and that God has purposes to unfold that are good, perfect, and pleasing. It may be that tragedy will strike our lives that day, as happened to Job, but God will not have been caught unaware. It may be that our plans will be altered and we end up in a foreign prison like Joseph, but God will have a purpose. It may be that you die on a Roman cross like the Lord Jesus, who prayed in the early hours of that very morning, "Not as I will, but as you will." But you can know this, that if you die today, you will die on time, and it won't be very long before you understand everything. Everything!

Isn't it good to know that such a positive and adventuresome attitude to life is designed to be part of the normal experience of every Christian? It is our willingness for this, to present our lives to Jesus Christ as wholly available to Him and expendable in His service, that gives us the right to call ourselves Christian. We will have this Man to "reign over us." Will you? Do you live each day on that basis?

5

A Change of Mind

After I had been preaching one evening, someone described my message as having been like offering someone a brand new car with an explanation of its many capabilities, but then forgetting to give him or her the ignition key and to explain how it works! I resolved never to do that again.

We have already stated that the Lord Jesus Christ is the focal point of the Christian life. As a perfect Man He demonstrated what a true man is supposed to be. In the first sermon preached after the church was born at Pentecost, the apostle Peter stressed this fact when he said, "Men of Israel, listen to this: Jesus of Nazareth was a man accredited by God to you by miracles, wonders, and signs, *which God did among you through him*, as you yourselves know" (Acts 2:22). It was as through a man that God worked through Jesus, and this is the explanation for all He ever said, did, and was, as we saw in chapter 2. Equally so, we have seen that it is God's activity within you and me that is to be the source of the quality of life we are called to live.

But how does this all come into being? How does God become operative within our lives? I trust this question has been provoked in your thinking as it was in the minds of the crowd of people who listened to Peter on the Day of Pentecost. Having preached the life, death, resurrection, exaltation, and lordship of Jesus Christ, the writer of the book of Acts states, "When the people heard this, they were cut to the heart and said to Peter and the other apostles, 'Brothers, what shall we do?'" (Acts 2:37). I find this interesting for the simple reason that Peter had not told them they could do anything! He had not told them they could be involved at all, he had only proclaimed to them the facts concerning Jesus Christ. But it was their very awareness of Jesus Christ that made them aware of their need to do something.

We have already defined *sin* as "missing the mark." The word *sin* therefore is a relative word, depending upon the target that has been missed. The target is the "glory of God" (Rom. 3:23) and this is the character of God which man, being made in God's image, was intended to express and reveal. Now, this glory has been made visible in the person and life of Jesus Christ, who is described as being "the radiance of God's glory and the exact representation of his being" (Heb. 1:3). It was in contrast to seeing the perfect Man, as Peter preached and described Him, that the people became aware of their own need.

This is an important fact to appreciate. It is only as people become conscious of Jesus Christ that they are able to recognize their own need. It is only as we see the glory of God in the life of Jesus Christ that we see our own need in its true perspective and recognize that we have fallen short of the glory of God. Peter testifies in his own experience that Christ called him "by his own glory and goodness" (2 Peter 1:3). In other words, it was the sheer goodness and glory of Christ, the expression of godliness in His life that made Him so utterly attractive and drew Peter to Him. This is why we must preach Christ—His life, His character, and His activities—because only as people see Him do they see themselves in the true light and become aware of the real nature of their sin and need. People rarely become aware of their sin by hearing someone preach sin to them. They become aware of their sin by the preaching of Christ, in contrast with whom they recognize their sin.

There was an advertisement on television in which a man came onto the screen wearing a white shirt that had just been washed in "ordinary" laundry detergent. He was smiling and relaxed as he confidently showed off his newly washed shirt. Then a second man came onto the screen wearing a shirt washed in some special laundry detergent which was about to be advertised. His shirt was a dazzling white, and he too, looked relaxed and confident. As he walked over and stood next to the man with the shirt washed in just ordinary laundry detergent, the other man's face began to fall. And seeing them stand together you could swear that the man with the shirt washed in ordinary detergent had a slightly gray shirt on! His grayness had been exposed by the brilliance of the second shirt. Had you gone to the first man earlier and said, "You have a dirty shirt on," he would have objected most strongly and let you know in no uncertain manner that it had just been washed that very morning in ordinary laundry detergent. But when he stood next to the man whose shirt had been washed in the special detergent, he came to an embarrassing conclusion: "I have a dirty shirt on."

I knew someone who maintained that when you talked to people about the Gospel, you should always begin with their sin. That, he believed, was their problem and until they faced it and were willing to deal with it, there was not much point in telling them anything else. So, in effect, his conversation with people would very soon lead to him saying something like, "Did you know that you are a dirty, filthy, stinking, miserable, rotten sinner?" He never seemed to get very far beyond that and used to end up being "persecuted for righteousness' sake," so he thought, and which I suspect he secretly enjoyed and saw as evidence that he had the Devil on the run! I have discovered that when you preach Christ and expose people to Him, to His life, to His work, and let them understand how He lived and why He lived as He did, it isn't long before some begin to say, "Do you know something? I think I am a dirty, filthy, stinking, miserable, rotten sinner." As we hold Christ up to people and we see the brilliance and beauty of His life, it is then that we become aware of our own grayness, if not blackness!

Some time ago I was visiting a school where I spoke to seventeen- and eighteen-year-olds for a double lesson lasting about one hour and twenty minutes. I began by posing the question, "Who is Christ?" and began to look at alternative explanations as to who He was. I then talked about the life He lived, the way He treated people, healed the sick, cared for the poor, the grounds on which He was arrested and tried, finally crucified, and that he then rose from the dead. From there we discussed the evidence for the Resurrection and the implications of a now risen and living Christ. At the conclusion it was lunch time, and one of the young men invited me to meet with some of them in a small conference room for lunch, where we could continue chatting. I was told there was a fish-and-chips shop across the road, and if I wished I could go and get some and come back and join them! As there didn't seem to be any other food available I did that, and when I got back into the conference room there were two young women present, one of them in tears. The one who was not crying said to me as I came in, "Look what you have done. You have upset my friend." I went across to them both and asked what had upset her. Between her sobs she said, "Why do you make us all feel so dirty? Why do you go on about

how bad everyone is?" I told her I could not recall talking about
how bad anyone was, had not mentioned dirt, and had made no
comments about anyone in the class. But I reminded her that I had
talked about how good and kind Jesus Christ was. I recognized
what was happening. As I had talked to the class, the Holy Spirit
had revealed to her who Christ really is, and as understanding of
Him dawned upon her, she found she was becoming increasingly
uncomfortable with herself. In contrast to Him, she was seeing her
sin. This is part of the Holy Spirit's task, to make us aware of our
sin by bringing into focus the Lord Jesus Christ, whose quality of
life we have come short of.

Had I gone into that class and condemned them for their sin, they
would have resisted, defended, and become highly indignant. Someone
has said that if you try to steal a bone from a dog, it will probably tear
you to pieces, but if you place a piece of juicy steak on the ground, it
will soon leave the bone and pick up the steak! When the Holy Spirit
exposes us to our sin, it is in order that it be dealt with, rejected, and
cleansed. But it is His job to "convict the world of guilt in regard to
sin" (John 16:8). Our job is to preach Christ, to lay out the "steak"
and to let people see Him. When the Holy Spirit does reveal sin, it is
not in order to condemn us or to humiliate us or to make us grovel in
our own dirt, but it is always as a prelude to cleaning us up and
equipping us for a new quality of life.

When Peter was asked by the crowd of people on the Day of
Pentecost, "What shall we do?" he gave them a very clear answer,
"Repent and be baptized, every one of you, in the name of Jesus
Christ so that your sins may be forgiven. And you will receive the
gift of the Holy Spirit" (Acts 2:38).

TURNING AROUND

Peter's first word of instruction to the people was "Repent." This
should not surprise us. The first word described as being preached
in the New Testament was in the statement of John the Baptist who
came "preaching in the Desert of Judea and saying, 'Repent, for the
kingdom of heaven is near'" (Matt. 3:1–2). Later, the first public
word from the lips of Jesus that has been recorded in the New
Testament was identical, "Repent, for the kingdom of heaven is
near" (Matt. 4:17). Peter gave this word of instruction on the day of
Pentecost, the day the church was born, and the people were provoked
to ask, "What shall we do?" "Repent" came the reply. Later, Paul

preaching in Athens announced, "In the past God overlooked such ignorance, but now he commands all people everywhere to repent" (Acts 17:30). Repentance then, spoken of as being "commanded" to "all people everywhere," is a key word in our response to God. There can be no avoiding the need to repent or compromising the command to repent, and any attempt to do so will short-circuit the work of God and bankrupt the blessing.

I have learned that, when counseling folks whose Christian lives have never come alive or seemed to be effective, it is often helpful to talk about repentance.

After a meeting in Scotland one evening, a young woman in her early twenties came to see me. She told me she had been a Christian for about two years, but that it just didn't seem to be working, despite her wanting it to do so. She attended church, but could not be enthusiastic like everyone else seemed to be. She tried reading her Bible but hardly ever got anything from it, and her prayers just hit the ceiling and fell dead on the floor. She wondered if the problem was that she hadn't been "chosen," and could I help her to find out. If she wasn't chosen (as she suspected), then she might as well drop the whole thing. I explained that whenever there seemed to be a problem in our relationship with God, it was never on His side but always on ours. I asked her if she would tell me a little about herself. She told me she had been brought up in a Christian home but at the age of eighteen had decided to leave. She was not a Christian at that stage, had no intention of becoming one, and had felt very resentful toward her upbringing and her church.

On leaving home she had joined a commune and had remained there for two years. At first she had really enjoyed herself and felt free for the first time in her life. No one was breathing down her neck to make sure she did what they thought she should, and she could live just as she wanted. But the enjoyment of that began to wear thin after a while, and she found herself becoming in bondage to other things she liked even less. After two years she ended up in a hospital. She did not explain to me the reasons for being there, but while there she began to think seriously about her life, where she was going, and what she was doing. She began to miss her family, and she told me how she began to realize that some of the people back at home and back at the church, with whom she had grown up, really had something, but the people with whom she now spent most of her time seemed as shallow as she felt inside. "Lying there in my hospital bed," she explained, "I decided that the Christian life was probably the right one after all, so I resolved to become a Christian and, when I left the hospital, to return to my parents and start again." This she did, asking Christ to become her Savior. But now that she was back at home, her Christian life had never come alive. She told me she did not believe verse 17 in 2 Corinthians 5 in which Paul wrote, "If anyone is in Christ, he is a new creation; the old has gone, the new has come," because not much of the old had gone, she could think of little of the new that had come, and as for being a "new creation" there didn't seem to be much difference. On hearing this, the obvious nonexistence of any real work of God in her life, I suggested that she had never really been born again because she had not come to a place of repentance. I pointed out that her motivation for coming home had been the same as her motivation for leaving in the first place. She wanted fulfillment, she wanted freedom, she wanted happiness, and it all centered around herself. "But I did ask Christ to come into my life, and I really meant it," she protested.

I am sure she did mean it, but her reasons for meaning it were not good ones. She was wanting Christ to be her servant. I explained to her that Christ does not come into a person's life just because He is asked. There are things that have to be dealt with that have created the barrier which has kept Him out until this time. That barrier, I tried to show her from Scripture, is our sin, our self-sufficiency, our independence. "Well I don't think that is my problem," she said. "I am desperate."

Our conversation by this time had lasted for an hour or so, and I felt I could see her problem very clearly. "You may be desperate," I acknowledged, "but what are you desperate for? For God, or for fulfillment? You have given no evidence of concern to meet God's requirements, and although you want Him to please you, I am not sure that you are equally concerned about pleasing Him. Your problem seems clear, you have never repented of your independence of God and of your sin."

"But I have," she insisted, "it is God who isn't doing His part." I have learned not to sympathize with a person's situation that throws a shadow onto the integrity and faithfulness of God, for He is never at fault. Our conversation was making the problem clearer all the time, and from all the details that had emerged, I felt sure enough to look her in the eye and say, "You have never repented, and until you do, you will not have a living relationship with God." I do not find it easy to speak as straight and directly to someone as that, and I trust it was said graciously and kindly. At that remark she stood up, "If this is the way you are going to talk to me I will not stay any longer," and at that she walked to the door and left, not even looking back to say good-bye!

The pastor of the church was still in the building waiting for me and I explained our conversation and how she had left in anger. He wasn't sure my diagnosis was right, but he hadn't been able to help her either, despite having talked at length to her several times.

The next evening as I stood up to preach, there at the back of the church was this woman. At the end of the service she came to talk to me again. I felt I had said all I could really say to her, so introduced her to a woman who would talk with her. About half an hour or so later, they both came to me. She had been crying. "Tonight I have repented," she said. She told me that she had gone home the previous evening feeling extremely angry with me. But deep down she knew her bluff had been called. She couldn't sleep all night, and all she could think of was "you haven't repented." Going to work on the train the next morning, the rhythm of the tracks had been saying, "You haven't repented." All day she had been in turmoil, but now she had told the Lord she was turning her back on her selfishness as best she knew how and would give Him the freedom to live His life in her for His purposes. She was about to discover that "whoever loses his life for me will find it" (Matt. 16:25) and that the fullness, the purpose, and the meaning she had longed for, but the demand for which she was now relinquishing, was about to become her experience. I saw her several times following that and she wrote to me on occasion. The last I heard she had gone to Southeast Asia to teach in a missionary school.

All of us are as near to God as we want to be. We may not be as close as we would like to be in that often we feel we would like to be closer, but we never actually meet the requirements and pay the price. Repentance is the response that enables God to get into business in our lives. So now we need to define the word more clearly. What exactly do we mean by *repentance*?

THINKING STRAIGHT

The Greek word translated "repent" in English is the word *metanoeo*. It is derived from two words, *meta* meaning "to change" and *nous* meaning "the mind." Quite simply, *repentance* means "to change the mind." It is not a feeling, but an attitude of mind, a thinking process. The key to God's working in our lives is in our thinking. "Do not conform any longer to the pattern of this world, but be transformed *by the renewing of your mind*," wrote Paul (Rom. 12:2). Solomon wrote of a man, "As he *thinketh* in his heart so is he" (Prov. 23:7, AV). It has been said that people are not what they think they are, but what they think, they are! Read that again carefully. In other words, what we *are* is a result of what we *think*. Repentance is a change of thinking. It is not just feeling bad about my sin or feeling good about God, but changing my thinking about both.

I have learned that tears are not a reliable indication of repentance. I have been involved with people who have shed bitter tears over their lives, their sin, and their failure, but who have not changed their minds about it, and consequently, despite their times of anguish, nothing changes.

Sin is very generous to the feelings. It can look good, sound good, and feel good. In fact, temptation is by definition attractive. If it were not attractive, it would not be temptation. If I disliked sin, I wouldn't have a problem with it, but my problem lies in the fact that I like it, and the only reason I commit sin is because either I enjoy it or it presents to me a good way out of a situation at the time. It is true that in due course I may feel very sorry and sad about it, but every sin I commit, I commit because at the time I wanted to, because it looked good and felt good. This is why I need to draw on the strength of God even in repentance.

Repentance is not a change of feeling toward sin (sin will go on appearing attractive) but it is a change of mind. If people will weep over their sin yet not change their minds about sin, they have not repented. On the other hand, people can change their minds about sin without ever shedding a tear, and they have repented.

I remember talking with a student at the end of a meeting I had been speaking at in the college he attended. We were halfway through a week-long mission conference sponsored by the Christian Union, and this student had come along out of curiosity. We talked together until late that evening and he seemed open and interested in the Gospel. Before I left him I explained that there is a cost to becoming a Christian and that he needed to face that honestly before making a response. The next evening I hoped he might be present at the meeting but he wasn't. However, on the following night he arrived early and told me he had been giving a lot of thought to what I had shared with him, but he felt he was unwilling to surrender his whole life to Jesus Christ and therefore had decided he could not become a Christian. I thanked him for his honesty and willingness to face realistically what was involved, but added that I would like to speak to him again and so we arranged that I would meet him later that evening.

Over a cup of coffee I acknowledged his honesty and realism in facing the cost of becoming a Christian, but now I wanted him to equally honestly and realistically face the cost of not becoming a Christian! We talked late into the night, and sometime long past midnight he said something like, "All right, you have persuaded me. If what you say is true, I haven't really got much choice, have I? I will become a Christian." It was very matter-of-fact, almost a cold decision. We prayed together and he told God that He could have his life from now on. I was unsure about how real this could have been. It was so matter-of-fact, so unemotional, so rational. But that night this student changed his mind. He changed his mind about God and gave God the right to be God in his life. He changed his mind about himself and, acknowledging his own inability to live as he should, he began to depend upon Christ within him. He changed his mind about his sin, confessed it to Christ, and thanked Him for taking it away on the cross. There seemed little emotion involved but there was a changed attitude. The following year he was elected as president of the Christian Union in his college. As I write this, he is shortly to graduate from a Bible college in the south of England to engage in a full-time pastoral and evangelistic ministry. As far as I know he did not get emotional about his sin, but he did change his mind about it. That is repentance.

A change of mind must lead to a change of behavior. If there is no change of behavior, it evidences there has been no change of mind. What we do reveals the truth of what we think. When John the Baptist came preaching repentance to people, there were certain things he exacted and demanded should accompany their change of mind.

"*Confessing their sins they were baptized by him in the Jordan River*" (Matt. 3:6). Confessing sin involves naming it, identifying it, and being specific about my rejection of it. Repentance, although a general attitude of mind toward God, myself, and sin, must be applied specifically. Naming our sin helps us to understand it too. If I tell lies, why do I tell lies? Am I trying to hide something? Am I too insecure to face truth in certain areas? James even encourages us to "confess your sins to each other" (James 5:16), and in that context he is talking about sin that has led to illness. There are physical, mental, and spiritual disorders that are a consequence of sin that needs identifying and confessing. Confession is not only necessary for forgiveness, but can in itself be therapeutic.

"Produce fruit in keeping with repentance" (Luke 3:8). Repentance must express itself in changed behavior patterns. John was specific about this. Luke records three groups of people who asked him how they could produce fruit in keeping with repentance—the crowd, the tax collectors, and then some soldiers. In his reply, John specifies three areas of their lives where repentance will be expressed—their social lives, business lives, and in their attitude to money.

Socially: "'What should we do then?' the crowd asked. John answered, 'The man with two tunics should share with him who has none, and the one who has food should do the same'" (Luke 3:10–11). The best indication of our true attitude toward God is found in our attitude toward people. Concerning Judgment Day, the Bible makes no mention of people being asked about their beliefs, but it speaks entirely of people being asked about their behavior, always their behavior toward other people and particularly toward those less privileged than themselves. We cannot escape that! Not that those good works have been the cause of salvation, but they are the effect of salvation, and the quality of our salvation is expressed in its effectiveness. In the parable of the sheep and the goats in Matthew 25, the basis on which the sheep are welcomed into the "kingdom prepared for you since the creation of the world" was their good works. "For I was hungry and you gave me something to eat, I was thirsty and you gave me something to drink, I was a stranger and you invited me in, I needed clothes and you clothed me, I was sick and you looked after me, I was in prison and you came to visit me" (Matt. 25:35–36). Conversely, to the goats He said, "Depart from me, you who are cursed, into the eternal fire prepared for the Devil and his angels. For I was hungry and you gave me nothing to eat, I was thirsty and you gave me nothing to drink, I was a stranger and you did not invite me in. I needed clothes and you did not clothe me, I was sick and in prison and you did not look after me" (Matt. 25:41–43). The whole point of that story is to show that our real attitude to Jesus Christ is shown in our attitude to other people, and the reality or otherwise of our repentance is seen in that area.

When people ask me how they can be sure they are Christians, I tell them that the evidence is in their behavior patterns. Books like 1 John and James are largely devoted to teaching us that. A social conscience is not something added on to the Christian life just because it happens to be the evangelical trend at present; it is a fundamental expression of the life of Jesus Christ within us if it is real and Christ is free.

In business: "Tax collectors also came to be baptized. 'Teacher,' they asked, 'what should we do?' 'Don't collect any more than you are required to,' he told them" (Luke 3:12–13). Repentance will be expressed in an integrity and honesty in our professional lives. The job of tax collecting was open to all sorts of abuse, and the collector could, and usually did, exploit those from whom he collected. It was so easy to do, and more so, people expected it. When the Lord Jesus had dealings with a tax collector named Zacchaeus, the first response Zacchaeus made was "Look, Lord! Here and now I give half of my possessions to the poor, and if I have cheated anybody out of anything, I will pay back four times the amount" (Luke 19:8). No wonder Jesus responded by saying, "Today, salvation has come to this house," because the evidence of his salvation was his changed attitude. A Christian at work should be the most trustworthy person on earth. Paul even encouraged slaves, of whom there were many in the Roman empire, "Serve wholeheartedly, as if you were serving the Lord, not men" (Eph. 6:7). That was not an endorsement of the practice of slavery, but instruction on how a Christian behaves should he find himself in that situation, as many did.

With money: "Then some soldiers asked him, 'And what should we do?' He replied, 'Don't extort money and don't accuse people falsely—be content with your pay'" (Luke 3:14). The other two areas are mentioned here too, their treatment of other people and their professional integrity, but he adds instruction about money. "Don't extort money . . . and be content with your pay." Money finds a new perspective in a repentant heart. "The love of money is a root of all kinds of evil," Paul told Timothy. "But you, man of God, flee from all this" (1 Tim. 6:10–11). Money is a very useful servant, but it is a terrible master. The rich young ruler was turned away by the Lord Jesus Christ because he was not willing to part with his money, and Jesus added to His bewildered disciples who were amazed at the conversation they had just witnessed, "How hard it is for the rich to enter the kingdom of God" (Mark 10:23).

There is a wonderful contentment in knowing all you need for all God plans He will provide, and the repentant person learns to be content. We could devote a whole chapter to what the Bible has to say about this. Suffice it here just to point out that according to John the Baptist, to be repentant is to be contented.

These are just some of the fruits of repentance. It is the behavior produced by repentance that God is concerned with. The Lord Jesus did not come into the world just to enable us to believe properly and get our doctrines right, but He came that on the basis of right believing there might be produced a behavior pattern that pleases Him. Belief is only a means to an end, the end product is our conduct. A change of mind *must* produce a change of behavior, or it can be denounced as false and will be among the "wood, hay, or straw" (1 Cor. 3:12) to be burned on Judgment Day.

repentance - contentment

6

Forgiveness and the Justice of God

Speaking on BBC radio, the head of a mental institution in Scotland made an astonishing observation. "If my patients could be assured of forgiveness, half of them could go home tomorrow," he claimed. An enormous number of mental breakdowns are a result of guilt that has never been dealt with. He put the figure as high as fifty percent.

Whatever else we may say about guilt, it is potentially destructive and we must learn to handle it. The psalmist David acknowledged the effect of guilt in his own experience when he wrote, "When I kept silent, my bones wasted away through my groaning all day long. For day and night your hand was heavy upon me; my strength was sapped as in the heat of summer" (Ps. 32:3–4). Guilt is heavy! Guilt is tiring! Guilt makes us groan! But how do we cope with it?

There are two main ways of coping with guilt. One is to redefine it so as to reduce the sense of personal responsibility and personal failure. Consequently, many psychologists spend much of their time looking for external factors as the cause of their clients' feelings of guilt. Having identified upbringing, parents, grandparents, neighbors, the church, the country, or the government as the cause, the victims can then vent their feelings by blaming and cursing these causes over which they had no responsibility and, having absolved themselves, begin to feel better for it. They must then learn to refuse to accept their feelings of guilt because they can now be classified as "false," deriving only from other people's mistreatment. This will then help them live more comfortably with themselves, and no doubt, superficially at least, it does. However, it doesn't actually solve the problem, it just relocates it.

The other way is to face up to guilt as a reality, accept responsibility for it, and cope with it from a position of responsibility. From a Christian point of view, having taken the second way, accepting responsibility for our guilt leads to us confessing it and receiving forgiveness. It is this forgiveness that is the first consequence of repentance. On the Day of Pentecost, after the crowds had asked, "What shall we do?" Peter replied, "Repent and be baptized everyone of you in the name of Jesus Christ so that your sins may be forgiven" (Acts 2:38). *Forgiveness* in these terms means that our guilt is erased. We are now regarded as "not guilty" of the sins of the past, and they will never be recalled against us or used as evidence to condemn us. That is a staggering claim, easy to accept as biblically and doctrinally correct, but hard to believe as being true for ourselves. Many people find forgiveness easy to be doctrinal about but hard to be practical about. They find it easy to believe in the possibility of other people's forgiveness but extremely difficult to believe in their own.

In the several years that I have been traveling, preaching, and counseling, I have been surprised at the number of Christians there are, some of many years standing, who have a suspicion that their forgiveness is not as all-embracing as they would like to believe. They have been constantly attacked by their own sense of guilt, sometimes confessing the same sins again and again but lacking the assurance of forgiveness.

A woman in her fifties once confessed to me that she had been involved in something particularly wrong while in her late teens, more than thirty years before. She had been a Christian at the time, and her sense of guilt had probably been heightened by that fact. For all those years she had lived with guilt from which she had not been able to find any liberty. She told me that most nights before she went to bed she would confess those thirty-year-old sins, but could not be sure they had been forgiven. She was a regular attender at her local church, but had never taken any responsibility because of her sense of unworthiness. She had declined several opportunities of becoming a Sunday school teacher, something of which she would have been capable, but which her sense of guilt forbade. Her sin had prevented her being a good wife and mother to her three children (in her opinion), and now she had been taken ill with a disease for which the doctors could promise her no cure. In her mind the reason was clear. The judgment of God was at last catching up with her. An extreme case? Not nearly as extreme as you might think. I have chosen to tell her story from among a number of people in a similar condition with whom I have had dealings and whose stories I could equally have told. Perhaps you identify with her. Behind the calm exterior of many Christians is the problem of unresolved guilt. Some are plagued by the fear they have committed the "unforgivable sin" (see Mark 3:29), and despite being Christians, they await the Judgment Day only with fear. I talked with that woman about the truths I want to share with you in these next pages.

CONVICTION OR CONDEMNATION?

There are two people who are concerned to talk to you about your sin. One is the Holy Spirit, the other is the Devil. With regard to the Holy Spirit, Jesus said, "When he comes, he will convict the world of guilt in regard to sin" (John 16:8). That is, without apology the Holy Spirit's work involves the bringing of conviction of sin. But the Devil holds another role. He is described as being "The accuser of our brothers" (Rev. 12:10), whose task is not to convict but to condemn. That verse goes on to specify that he "accuses them before our God day and night." In other words, he is forever telling tales to God about you and me with the object of blackening our motives and condemning our characters. (For an example, see Job 1:9–11, in which he accuses Job of wrong motives for godliness). As he accuses us in the presence of God, he will certainly accuse us to ourselves too.

There is a big difference between the conviction of the Holy Spirit and the condemnation of the Devil. Condemnation throws our guilt on us like a wet blanket that smothers us and leaves us with no means of breaking free. Conviction makes us aware of our sin, but at the same time makes us aware of the way out and the possibility of forgiveness. The Holy Spirit exposes our sin not in order to condemn us, but always in order to liberate us and to clean us up. When our consciousness of sin leaves us feeling persistently hopeless and condemned, with no way out and no prospect other than having to live with it, it is satanic in origin. Some of us have a problem here in that we are much more ready to understand the Devil's values than we are God's! We find it much easier to believe the bad news than we do the good news. We hold an intrinsic attitude toward ourselves that is negative and too ready to assume wrong, to accept guilt, and to feel condemned, rather than to believe in forgiveness, to accept righteousness, and to enjoy liberty. I am not saying this to undermine the reality of sin or the seriousness of guilt, but to show that these are not the last words in our vocabulary. Sin has been dealt with, guilt can be erased!

I know someone who if, when she is driving her car through town, she hears somone blow a horn she will instinctively assume it is being blown at her, and that she has done something wrong. There may be fifty cars in the area at the time but the assumption is that it is at her the horn is being blown, and that whatever is wrong will have been her fault. Does it surprise you when I say that for a long time she had an enormous problem coping with guilt? She was a Christian, but as a person always down on herself, she naturally assumed that God was always down on her too. Satan will capitalize on that negative attitude and will have little difficulty keeping one in a perpetual state of fear and guilt.

The Devil is called a liar. Jesus said of him, "He was a murderer from the beginning, not holding to the truth, for there is no truth in him. When he lies, he speaks his native language, for he is a liar and the father of lies" (John 8:44). The only time he does not tell lies is when he talks to us about our sin, for most of us recognize that the truth is bad enough. However, the lie is to take that sin from under the blood of Christ where it has been dealt with, cleansed, forgiven, and forgotten, and re-expose it to us in order to condemn us. Interestingly, the Devil does not condemn us while outside of Christ. He doesn't need to, for he specializes in lies, and outside of Christ sin is condemned and there is no forgiveness. In any case, it would be counterproductive to create a conscience in people who have been content to live with their sin. It might make them look for forgiveness. But the moment we come to Christ and are forgiven, Satan's deceitful nature is to dig up what God has buried and use it as ammunition to condemn us and to destroy our freedom and joy in being forgiven.

THE BASIS OF FORGIVENESS

One of the barriers to our enjoying forgiveness is lack of understanding of it. What is the basis within the character of God, whom we recognize to be holy and righteous, that enables Him to forgive my sin? I have on several occasions when speaking to a group of people about this asked them to indicate whether they believe God forgives us on the basis of His *mercy* or on the basis of His *justice*. Is it because He is being generous and kind toward us, or is it because He is being absolutely right and just toward us? It is not surprising that the majority indicate it is on the basis of mercy that God forgives. But they are wrong! God forgives us on the basis of His justice. "If we confess our sins, he is faithful and *just* and will forgive us our sins and purify us from all unrighteousness" (1 John 1:9). If God was to forgive us only on the basis of His mercy, the Cross would not have been necessary. It is the death of Christ on the cross that makes forgiveness by God a just act. It is in appealing to His justice that forgiveness is possible, not in appealing to His mercy. Let me try to explain this.

Justice and mercy appear in themselves to be incompatible. To exercise justice and mercy toward the same person at the same time in regard to the same thing is not possible. If I went to court to face a charge of breaking the speed limit in my car and was found to be guilty, the judge would have two options. He could either deal with me mercifully and let me go free, or he could deal with me justly and enforce the penalty of my misdemeanor. But he could not do both. If he was merciful toward me and, concluding my behavior had been entirely out of character, chose to let me go free, he could not then at the same time be just and impose a fine. Or, if he chose to be just and insist on my paying a penalty, he could not at the same time be merciful. The two are incompatible with each other.

Just imagine that despite a desire on the part of the judge to be merciful, he senses his obligation as judge, and having carefully weighed the details of my offense, he imposes a fine of fifty dollars. That would be an entirely just act, and my ability to be free and to have my crime removed from the police records as an offense would now be upon payment of a fine. Stretch your imagination to suppose that the judge himself, out of sheer kindness and mercy toward me, then stepped from his bench and with checkbook in hand, paid my fifty-dollar fine. The records of that courtroom would indicate that I had been found guilty of my crime, had had a fine of fifty dollars imposed, and that the fine had been paid. The attitude of the judge toward me would have been one of mercy and kindness, as it was this that motivated him to pay my fine. But I do not leave the courtroom a free man in the eyes of the law because of an act of mercy; I leave a free man because justice has been done. The fine is paid and I am legally free. That may be a simple illustration, but do you see the point? It is on the basis of justice that I am made free!

It is perfectly true that in the heart of God it was His love and mercy toward us that made the Cross an event in history. "For God so loved the world that he gave his one and only Son" (John 3:16), but having sent Christ, who died upon the cross as our substitute, it is now on the basis of justice that God deals with our sin. Peter states, "For Christ died for sins once for all, the righteous for the unrighteous, to bring you to God" (1 Peter 3:18). With the demands of His law satisfied, God is legally and morally obligated to forgive us! This is the basis on which we claim and accept forgiveness. It is not a presumption to believe my sin is forgiven, but it is on the basis of the justice and integrity of God that I hold it to be true.

When I leave the courtroom after the judge has paid my fine, although I have not paid a penny, I leave legally and justly. No one has the right to detain me and insist I make a contribution, for were I to contribute an additional fifty cents, just to ease my conscience a little, the books would become unbalanced. The fine would be recorded as fifty dollars, but the penalty paid would be fifty dollars and fifty cents. This is why penance is unnecessary. To insist on any form of penance is to undermine the sufficiency of the work of Christ. I cannot contribute to the penalty paid for my sin, neither do I need to, for payment has been made in full. Therefore on the basis of God's justice I can be forgiven.

As long as I think of forgiveness as the result of God being merciful to me, I am left with the realization that there is no moral obligation on God's part to forgive. Therefore I may conclude that I have sinned once too often, have exhausted His mercy, and whereas He may have forgiven me before, He is unlikely to do so again. It is this that lies at the base of the continuous sense of guilt experienced by so many. In effect, as they think of God's dealings with their sin, they are bypassing the Cross and its significance. The Devil will attack the sufficiency and the efficacy of the Cross, for on the Cross sin was destroyed and through the Cross Satan was doomed. The tragedy is that many do not believe that.

God forgives because He is just, and therefore for God not to forgive would be unjust and immoral. To question God's forgiveness is to question His justice and moral integrity. We must never, and need never, do that.

May I remind you, of course, that there are conditions to experiencing forgiveness. Peter stated, "Repent . . . so that your sins may be forgiven" (Acts 2:38). John wrote, "If we confess our sins, he is faithful and just and will forgive us our sins" (1 John 1:9). Jesus said in the Sermon on the Mount, "If you forgive men when they sin against you, your heavenly Father will also forgive you. But if you do not forgive men their sins, your heavenly Father will not forgive your sins" (Matt. 6:14–15). Scripture is clear that we need to confess our sins and repent of them before God, and we must extend the same forgiveness toward others that we anticipate God will show toward us. I cannot receive forgiveness from God while refusing to forgive someone else. Jesus made that very clear, and in the Lord's Prayer He taught us to say, "Forgive us our debts, *as we* have forgiven our debtors" (Matt. 6:12). Therefore we have no right to expect forgiveness if we are unforgiving to someone else. In fact, our being willing to forgive others is part of our repentance.

THE UNFORGIVABLE SIN

There are some Christian people whose lives are haunted by a terrible fear. The fear is that they have committed the "unforgivable sin." They fear that all will not be well for them on Judgment Day, and in the meantime they are to be restricted in their usefulness to God, having been spiritually maimed. Jesus spoke about an unforgivable sin, and it has been recorded for us by Matthew, Mark, and Luke. In the words of Mark, "Whoever blasphemes against the Holy Spirit will never be forgiven; he is guilty of an eternal sin" (Mark 3:29). The issue is our understanding of what is meant by "blasphemes against the Holy Spirit." The context of this statement was the persistent refusal of the scribes to recognize the working of the Holy Spirit in the life of Jesus, and instead, they attributed His miraculous powers to Beelzebub, the prince of demons.

It is always important to understand the particular statements of Scripture in the light of their wider context of the whole Scripture. This is particularly important when the statement in question would appear to be saying something that is out of the spirit of the whole of the Bible. The Bible is a unit, and it must be as part of the unit that we try to understand the details, remaining always on our guard against taking a text out of its context and using it as a pretext for something that is not true!

Elsewhere in the Bible, forgiveness is spoken of as encompassing all of our sin. John wrote, "the blood of Jesus . . . cleanses us from *all* sin" (1 John 1:7) and "If we confess our sins, he is faithful and just and will forgive us our sins and purify us from *all* unrighteousness" (1 John 1:9). Paul wrote, "There is now *no* condemnation for those who are in Christ Jesus" (Rom. 8:1). It is important to note that there is no exception clause written into these verses, that is, "cleanses us from all sin, unless you happen to be guilty of the unforgivable sin, in which case you will still be guilty of that"! No, forgiveness of sin is spoken of as all-inclusive, and there is no allowance made anywhere for someone who is only partially forgiven because of their guilt of something that is unforgivable. This must be significant.

The only means of forgiveness is the application of the death of Christ in response to the convicting work of the Holy Spirit. It is the Spirit who makes us aware of our sin and who points us to the way out of our sin through Christ. To resist the working of the Holy Spirit therefore is to close any way of obtaining forgiveness, which is exactly what the scribes were doing when Jesus warned them of the possibility of unforgiveness. They were so hardened against Jesus that, even acknowledging the supernatural element in His ministry, they would rather attribute it to a demon than to the Spirit of God. To resist and to blaspheme the Spirit in this way was to close off any possibility of forgiveness. Thus, the unforgivable sin is not an act that one can commit in a moment with no possibility of erasing it, but it is a refusal to accept the only means of obtaining forgiveness and, in thus resisting the Holy Spirit, choose to remain in one's sin, unforgiven, and with no other possibility of cleansing.

It is for this reason that a person who is already a Christian cannot be guilty of such a thing, for his very response to the Holy Spirit that enabled him to become a Christian is his refusal to be guilty. If as a Christian you fear being guilty of an unforgivable sin, do not take the verse that condemns you out of the context of Scripture as a whole, but rather, rejoice in the all-encompassing nature of God's forgiveness toward you. Then begin to believe and live as though you are clean—for clean you are!

WHAT GOD DOES WITH OUR SIN

There are some vividly descriptive verses in the Bible which tell us what God does with our sin. These could be extremely encouraging for us to think about.

As far as the east is from the west, so far has he removed our transgressions from us (Ps. 103:12). This is a beautiful picture. He does not speak of our sin being removed as far as the north is from the south, but as far as the "east is from the west." North and south are fixed points, east and west are not. Recently I flew from London to Japan. On leaving London we flew north, covering the full length of mainland Britain, passing by the Orkney Islands off northern Scotland and eventually over the arctic circle. We were flying in a straight line, but it wasn't too long before, having crossed the most northerly point, we found ourselves traveling south across Alaska, touching down in Anchorage, then heading in a southwesterly direction to Tokyo. The north is a fixed point, and so is the south. But not so the east and west. You could set off by air in a westerly direction and keep going right around the world coming back to the same spot from which you left without ever having to go east. Similarly you could fly directly east, go right around the world without having to go west. East and west are nonexistent points, and it is as far as these nonexistent points are away from each other that God has removed our transgressions from us. Isn't that a wonderful picture? We and our sin have been separated from each other to irreconcilable positions! Therefore, as a forgiven sinner, do not attempt to restore your sin, and firmly resist any attempts of the Devil to bring about a reconciliation.

You had put all my sins behind your back (Isa. 38:17). This is another very graphic picture. If God is omnipresent (in all places at all times) where is there such a place as behind His back? Wherever it is, it is so far as to be outside space and in a place which, by definition, is beyond anything that exists! You may feel I am taking the picture too literally, and it just means that our sin has been taken out of God's reckoning, rather than put literally behind His back. You are probably right if you think that, but the picture is a very graphic one of the infinity of distance to which God has taken our sin.

I, even I, am he who blots out your transgressions, for my own sake, and remembers your sins no more (Isa. 43:25). God has a unique ability. He not only forgives, but He also forgets or more precisely, He remembers no more. I was confused by this at one stage. If God forgets our sin, I reasoned, and we talk about our past sin to someone, God may think we are telling lies, because He has forgotten! However, the truth is not that He forgets but that He remembers no more. That is, the God who knows all things will never recall what He knows about me, never call me to account for it, never use it as ammunition against me, and never condemn me for it. He will remember it no more and treat me as though my sin never took place. We have the ability to forgive but do not have the ability to forget as readily. I remember on one occasion preaching in New York City in a church in the Bowery area of downtown Manhattan. The place was full and around halfway through the message, a man who had been sitting at the end of his row and against the wall stood up. He looked down the row as though he wanted to get out, but no one made any move to let him pass by. After a moment or so, someone stood up behind him, tapped him on the shoulder, and whispered in a voice loud enough for me to hear, "Sit down, you are blocking my view." The man in front turned around and whispered equally as loud, "I am trying to get out." "Then get out or sit down," the other responded, "but please don't just stand there." At this, the man in front clenched his fist, swung round, caught the man behind with a resounding thump, knocked him over, and then knelt on his own seat, reached over, and gave him another one! Two or three men in the church quickly grabbed him, and the last I saw he was being forcefully marched out through the doors at the back.

At the conclusion of the service, the man asked to come back in and apologize to me for disrupting my meeting. When he was eventually brought to me, he explained he had been drinking and wasn't acting normally (I had concluded the first and wondered about the second!) and asked if I would forgive him. I did, and I meant it. But just imagine that on the next evening I was about to begin to preach when suddenly the doors swung open and in walked that man. A little voice inside me would say, "Watch out, here comes trouble!" Why? Because I hadn't forgiven him? No, I had forgiven him. But I hadn't forgotten. If I met him close up again, I would be careful to stay just far enough away should he decide to swing a right hook! Although I have the capacity to forgive, I do not have the capacity to remember no more. God does. He does not treat me as the failure or sinner I was. The past that has been cleansed means nothing to Him now. It has gone, and He treats me, and you, as though our sins never took place. This is the extent of forgiveness.

There is now no condemnation for those who are in Christ Jesus (Rom. 8:1). This is the extent to which God remembers our sin no more! This verse is in the present tense. Today, there is no condemnation, and God has nothing against me. The conflict is over, the guilt has been taken away, and I am not condemned. Remember that whenever a Christian feels condemned, it is satanic in origin and not of God. In this area, Satan must be resisted.

Love is made complete among us so that we will have confidence on the day of judgment, because in this world we are like him (1 John 4:17). This is a remarkable verse. The extent to which the love of God has reached into our lives is that on the Judgment Day we will not come into the presence of God cowering and fearful, dreading the encounter, but humbly, boldly, and confidently. Why? John says that the full extent of the love of God for us is expressed in the fact that "in this world, we are like him." We will stand in the presence of the Father as pure and righteous as the Lord Jesus Christ, and as the Father would welcome the Son, so He will welcome you and me.

Why is this so? Have we earned it? Of course not. But there was a day in history when the skies turned black and the Father turned His back on the Son as that pure, holy, righteous Son of God became sin. All of my filth, failure, and sin was heaped upon the Lord Jesus, and, in exchange, all of His goodness and purity has been poured out upon me as I became a forgiven sinner. Paul put it this way, "God made him who had no sin to be sin for us, so that in him we might become the righteousness of God" (2 Cor. 5:21). What an exchange! The *Living Bible* paraphrases it like this, "For God took the sinless Christ and poured into him our sin. Then in exchange, he poured God's goodness into us." He took our sin, and we take His righteousness. Does that thrill you and humble you? Do not let the Devil rob you of the enjoyment of a full cleansing of your sin.

But, wonderful as it is to be forgiven and to be clean, that is not the whole point of the Christian life! Jesus Christ did not come into the world in order just to clean us up. Cleansing us is necessary and wonderful, but getting rid of sin is only a means to an end. It is so that the real purpose of our forgiveness might take place, and it is to that we will now turn.

7

The Spirit Within You

The purpose of the work of Jesus Christ is something more than to forgive us our guilt and cleanse us from our sin. That certainly meets one of the deepest needs that people have, as we have discussed in the previous chapter. However, man does not just have a need for forgiveness, but also a hunger for goodness. A person's consciousness of guilt derives from his desire to be good, and it is the establishment of goodness that is the purpose of the work of Christ. Christ forgives us our sin, not because being clean is the end product of His work, but in order that He might come and live His life within us by the Holy Spirit. It is the coming of the Holy Spirit, on the basis of one's cleansing, that actually makes one a Christian.

A person is not a Christian because his or her sin has gone, but because the Holy Spirit has come! Paul wrote, "If anyone does not have the Spirit of Christ, he does not belong to Christ" (Rom. 8:9). If I went into a bookshop to purchase a book costing five dollars, two things would take place. I would hand over the five dollars, and I would receive the book. If, as I left the shop, I was stopped by a friend who asked me what I had been doing, I would not reply, "I have been giving away five dollars." That would be a perfectly true statement, but I would reply, "I have been buying a book." In order to do that I had given away five dollars, but the giving of the money was only a means to the end and was not in itself the object of the exercise! My purpose was to acquire the book.

In a similar way, vital and wonderful as it is to be forgiven for our sin (and not for one moment do we belittle the significance of that), that is neither what makes us Christians nor fulfills the purpose of being Christians. It is only a means to the end. It makes possible the coming of the Holy Spirit into the life of the forgiven person to live the life of Jesus Christ within and reproduce the character of

Jesus Christ through him or her. This is why it is sad to meet Christians who, while being very grateful for their forgiveness, have never got around to enjoying the purpose of their forgiveness by living in the energy of the Holy Spirit. It is almost like being aware of having given away five dollars, yet not be enjoying the book, or like even forgetting that this was the purpose of the exercise!

On Calvary, Christ dealt with our need for forgiveness when He died on the cross, but at Pentecost, He dealt with our need for power and godliness when the Holy Spirit was made freely available to anyone prepared to meet the conditions upon which they could receive Him. It is His presence within one's life that makes one a Christian.

WHO IS THE HOLY SPIRIT?

Who is He? It is interesting that throughout Scripture the Holy Spirit is not given a personal name but is described only in terms of His work. He is called, "the Spirit of truth" (John 16:13), "the Counselor" (John 14:26), "the Holy Spirit," and several other titles. Both the Father and the Son are given personal names, such as Yahweh and Elohim for the Father, Jesus and Emmanuel for the Son, but the Spirit remains anonymous as to His personal identity. We will comment on the possible significance of that later, but for now I want to suggest that this omission has led some to think of the Holy Spirit as being less than a person. He is sometimes thought of as a power or a force or an influence which we need to tap and make use of in the way that wind can be used to fly a kite or steam to drive an engine or water to run a hydroelectric generator. But this is not adequate. Although sometimes the Holy Spirit is described as being like wind or like fire (in fact, both the Hebrew and the Greek words for "Spirit" in the Old and New Testaments are the same as the words for "wind"), we must not see Him as *something* but as *someone*. He is a person. The composite qualities of personality are the abilities to think, to feel, and to decide. That is, to possess a mind, emotions, and a will. The Holy Spirit does not have a physical body, and neither does the Father, but personality is not a physical attribute, it is the combination of these three qualities.

1. *The Holy Spirit thinks*: "For who among men knows the thoughts of a man except the man's spirit within him? In the same way none knows the thoughts of God except the Spirit of God. We have not received the spirit of the world but the Spirit who is from

God, that we may understand what God has freely given us" (1 Cor. 2:11–12). If the Holy Spirit is the one who both knows the thoughts of God and who reveals and teaches them to us, it indicates His ability to think. In the few verses preceding these, Paul is saying that God's truth is not known just by *observation:* "No eye has seen, no ear has heard," nor by *meditation:* "No mind has conceived what God has prepared for those who love him," but by *revelation:* "But God has revealed it to us by his Spirit" (1 Cor. 2:9–10). Revelation is the Spirit's task in the world. Prophecy came from men "carried along by the Holy Spirit" (2 Peter 1:21), and often in Scripture we find the Spirit speaking to people.

2. *The Holy Spirit feels*: The Scripture speaks of the Holy Spirit experiencing both positive and negative emotions. "I urge you, brothers, by our Lord Jesus Christ and by the love of the Spirit, to join me in my struggle by praying to God for me" (Rom. 15:30). Not only does the Spirit Himself love, but one of His marks in our experience is to produce such positive emotions as love, joy, and peace. I know that each of these qualities is something more than just emotion, but none of them can be detached from feeling.

The Spirit experiences negative emotions too. Paul warned the Ephesian Christians, "Do not grieve the Holy Spirit of God" (Eph. 4:30). He can be hurt, grieved, and saddened. I once heard George B. Duncan say that "We grieve the Holy Spirit when we fail to allow Him to do in us that for which He was given to us." It is a sobering thought to realize that we can bring either joy or sadness to God the Spirit. He can look upon us and be glad, or He can look upon us and be grieved. When I love God with all my heart, soul, strength, and mind, there is no greater incentive to holy living than to know it is possible to bring Him pleasure and to avoid at all costs that which brings Him pain.

3. *The Holy Spirit decides*: Speaking of spiritual gifts, Paul writes, "All these are the work of one and the same Spirit, and he gives them to each one, just as he determines" (1 Cor. 12:11). It is the Holy Spirit's prerogative to give His gifts as He chooses, something He shares with both the Father and the Son. This is why we do not have the right to insist on particular spiritual gifts either for ourselves or for others but must recognize His freedom to give as He desires.

Throughout the Bible the Holy Spirit engages in activities that are possible only to a personal being:

He speaks: "While they were worshiping the Lord and fasting, the Holy Spirit said, 'Set apart for me Barnabas and Saul for the work to which I have called them'" (Acts 13:2). Many times the Spirit is spoken of as speaking. How He speaks is His own business! It would be dangerous to limit Him to certain areas or to expect Him to speak only in predictable ways. Suffice it to say, when God wants you or me to know something, it will be the Holy Spirit's task to tell it to us in whatever way suits Him.

He teaches: Jesus said of Him, "The Counselor, the Holy Spirit, whom the Father will send in my name, will teach you all things and will remind you of everything I have said to you" (John 14:26). When we want to learn of Christ and to know the things God wants us to know, it is in a humble dependence upon the Holy Spirit that He becomes our teacher.

He intercedes: "The Spirit helps us in our weakness. We do not know what we ought to pray, but the Spirit himself intercedes for us with groans that words cannot express . . . the Spirit intercedes for the saints in accordance with God's will" (Rom. 8:26–27). That is such an encouraging promise. There are times when we have no idea of how we should pray. But the Holy Spirit takes the burden that is on our hearts, and He interprets it to the Father, putting it through the sifting of God's will, so that our burden and our groanings become an intelligent prayer, wholly consistent with the will of God.

He guides: Jesus promised of the Spirit that "he will guide you into all truth" (John 16:13). This does not mean that truth will just appear in our minds out of heaven! The operative word is *guide*. As we diligently study the Bible and think carefully and clearly about its truth, the Spirit will guide our thinking and bring us into all truth. You can only guide something that is moving, and the idea that the Spirit will just give us truth from nowhere is not implied in this verse at all, but it is as we are actively engaged in seeking for truth.

He commands: "Paul and his companions traveled throughout the region of Phrygia and Galatia, having been kept by the Holy Spirit from preaching the word in the province of Asia. When they came to the border of Mysia, they tried to enter Bithynia, but the Spirit of Jesus would not allow them to" (Acts 16:6–7). There we have the interesting situation of the Holy Spirit forbidding Paul and his friends to preach! The right to preach or do anything is not that the activity in itself is good, but that the Holy Spirit has sent us and we are operating under His authority. He must be the strategist in our lives and work, and we must give Him the right to give us our direction.

He appoints: Paul told the elders at the church in Ephesus, "Guard yourselves and all the flock of which the Holy Spirit has made you overseers. Be shepherds of the church of God, which he bought with his own blood" (Acts 20:28). The church is not intended to be a democracy where the leaders do what the majority of the people want, but a theocracy where the leaders implement what God wants. In the Bible the majority were almost always wrong! A church run on democratic principles is almost bound to come into conflict with the will of God sooner or later. Leaders, as at Ephesus, are to be godly people who spend time listening to Him and implementing His plans and program. Paul reminds the Ephesian elders that it is the Holy Spirit who appointed them to their leadership.

He can be insulted: The book of Hebrews talks about the deserving punishment of someone who tramples the Son of God under foot, "and who has insulted the Spirit of grace" (Heb. 10:29). You can desecrate an object, but you can only insult a person. The Spirit can be insulted.

He can be lied to: "Then Peter said, 'Ananias, how is it that Satan has so filled your heart that you have lied to the Holy Spirit. . . . you have not lied to men but to God'" (Acts 5:3–4). You will remember the story of how Ananias and his wife, Sapphira, agreed to give the impression to the church in Jerusalem that they were giving sacrificially when they were not. Peter describes it as lying to the Holy Spirit.

All of these qualities teach us that the Holy Spirit is a person who thinks and acts freely and independently and who is capable of feeling both joy and pain.

Before going any further we must acknowledge one important conclusion to which this brings us. Because the Holy Spirit is a person, we must not think of Him as a power to be used or exploited. If we do think of Him in impersonal terms, we will be tempted to think of Him as something to be used, to take advantage of in the way I might think of making use of the electricity supply to my home to accomplish all sorts of things. But seeing Him as a person causes us to ask not "How can I use Him?" but "How can He use me?" He is not there to be ordered but to be obeyed. His work is not to give us power to do our thing, but to give us the privilege of being another channel through which He does His things!

THE HOLY SPIRIT IS GOD

If it is established that the Holy Spirit is a person, it must also be recognized that the Holy Spirit is God. He is not just a servant of God or an agent of God, but He is God. I will list four things that indicate His deity:

1. *He receives divine acclaim*: When Ananias and his wife tried to deceive the apostles in Jerusalem, Peter told them, "You have lied to the Holy Spirit. . . . you have not lied to men but to God" (Acts 5:3–4). The Holy Spirit was called "God" by Peter. There were times too when the New Testament writers felt free to substitute the title "Holy Spirit" for "Lord" when quoting from the Old Testament and in this way indicated their clear identification of the Old Testament God with the Holy Spirit. (For examples of this, compare Jer. 31:33 with Heb. 10:15 and Isa. 6:8–10 with Acts 28:8–10).

2. *He possesses divine attributes:* There are qualities the Holy Spirit possesses that belong exclusively to God:

He is all-powerful (*omnipotent*): The angel Gabriel was sent to Mary to announce that she would give birth to the Messiah, and when she questioned the possibility of this, as she was a virgin, he replied, "The Holy Spirit will come upon you, and the power of the Most High will overshadow you. . . . For nothing is impossible with God" (Luke 1:35–37). Twice in the New Testament the statement is made that "nothing is impossible with God," once in relation to physical birth when the promise was made to Mary, and once in relation to spiritual birth when the disciples asked Jesus who could be saved if the demands were so high that He had sent the rich young ruler away empty-handed. To Mary it was promised that the doing of the impossible was the task of the Holy Spirit.

He is all-knowing (*omniscient*): Paul wrote of Him, "the Spirit searches all things, even the deep things of God . . . no one knows the thoughts of God except the Spirit of God" (1 Cor. 2:10–11). No one teaches the Holy Spirit anything! It is wonderful to know that the Spirit who indwells us is One who knows everything there is to know, who will never be taken by surprise or caught unaware of, or unprepared for, any event that we pass through. What we do not know, the Holy Spirit does, and as He lives within us to guide us in the fulfilling of God's purposes, there need be no accidents. He will always be one step ahead of our circumstances.

He is in all places (*omnipresent*): David wrote, "Where can I go from your Spirit? Where can I flee from your presence? If I go up to the heavens, you are there; if I make my bed in the depths, you are there. If I rise on the wings of the dawn, if I settle on the far side of the sea, even there your hand will guide me, your right hand will hold me fast" (Ps. 139:7–10). The whole of this psalm is a testimony to the far-reaching concern of God for men. David tells how God has "searched" him and known him and is familiar with all of his ways. Even before his birth God has seen him and planned him and has a book in which He has written his days before they came to be. But in the middle of the psalm, David describes the impossibility of escaping from the presence of the Holy Spirit. None can ever place themselves in a position that is out of His reach. The farther a person runs, the bigger he or she discovers God to be! That is why it is not always a tragedy when people run away from God. In their running, He teaches them about His bigness. Jonah discovered that when he ran away from God's instructions to him, God was behind all the events that eventually had him in a corner and left him with little option but to get right with God again.

He is eternal: To be eternal is to have no beginning and no end. A Christian is everlasting (that is, he has no end) because he has received eternal life, which is the life of the eternal God, whose presence in us assures us that although we had a beginning in time, we will have no end. It is God's life that is eternal, and it is the gift of God to us (not the gift *from* God) that is our eternal life. God is the gift, and upon receiving His presence and life, we begin to enjoy His eternal life.

The Holy Spirit is described as being eternal. "How much more, then, will the blood of Christ, who through the eternal Spirit offered himself unblemished to God, cleanse our consciences from acts that lead to death, so that we may serve the living God" (Heb. 9:14).

3. *He performs divine activities*: There are a number of activities attributed to the Holy Spirit that we know belong exclusively to God:

He creates: The Holy Spirit is mentioned in the opening statement of the Bible. With the earth formless and empty, "the Spirit of God was hovering over the waters" (Gen. 1:2). The psalmist writes, "When you send your Spirit, they are created, and you renew the face of the earth" (Ps. 104:30). The whole of the Trinity was involved in Creation, as they are together in most major events. Dr. G. Campbell Morgan in his book *The Spirit of God* suggests the idea that the will of God was expressed in the Word of God but fulfilled by the Spirit of God. The Father expresses His mind and purpose in His Son, described as the "Word of God" (John 1:1), but it is implemented by the Spirit who brings it into being. The primary purpose of this study is to discover who it is that comes to live within the lives of forgiven sinners. I would remind you that if part of the Holy Spirit's job in the past has been to create something out of nothing, then to create something out of your life is not going to be His most difficult task! I am frustrated by people I talk to who have no difficulty believing that God could create the universe but who do have difficulty believing God can do something worthwhile with them. The one who brought things into being in the first place will live within you and make your life His workshop.

He regenerates: Jesus said, "Unless a man is born of water and the Spirit, he cannot enter the kingdom of God" (John 3:5). Paul wrote, "And if the Spirit of him who raised Jesus from the dead is living in you, he who raised Christ from the dead will also give life to your mortal bodies through his Spirit, who lives in you" (Rom. 8:11). It is never the task of a human being to make someone else a Christian. That is an impossibility. All we can do is introduce people to Jesus Christ and He alone has the ability to give new life to them. C. H. Spurgeon, the famous London preacher of the nineteenth century, one day had a drunk man pointed out to him on the street and was told mockingly by one of his antagonists that this drunk had been one of his converts. Spurgeon replied that he looked like one of his converts, but he certainly was not one of God's! No preacher has ever converted anyone. His job is simply to make Jesus Christ clear, and as people respond to Christ, the Holy Spirit does the job of converting and regenerating. That is why, if the preacher moves on, the converts don't collapse if he has faithfully pointed them to Christ.

He is sovereign: Speaking of spiritual gifts as being the work of the Holy Spirit, Paul writes, "He gives them to each man, just as he determines" (1 Cor. 12:11). Spiritual gifts are not toys to be played with but tools to be worked with. The Holy Spirit will give to the church the abilities that are needed to fulfill the plans of the Lord Jesus Christ who is its Head. Spiritual gifts are for the church and for its general upbuilding, not for individuals to exercise in their own corners. It is the Holy Spirit who exercises sovereignty in giving as He determines.

He is the Author of prophecy: Peter writes, "For prophecy never had its origin in the will of man, but men spoke from God as they were carried along by the Holy Spirit" (2 Peter 1:21). Peter is almost certainly writing about the written prophets of the Old Testament and stating why the Scriptures are so utterly reliable. They are reliable and to be trusted not because of their content but because of their origin. We do not take the Bible seriously because of what it says but because of who is saying it. If we accept the Bible because we happen to like what it says, we are in no more virtuous a position than those who reject the Bible because they do not like what it says. Our basis for rejecting or accepting has been the same. We accept the Bible because it is the Word of God. He is speaking. He is revealing Himself and His purpose, and whether we happen to like what He says or not is a secondary issue. The Holy Spirit has been involved in its compilation as men of God were "carried along by the Holy Spirit."

The Holy Spirit performs divine activities; in fact, whenever God does something great, the Holy Spirit is active. Whether it is the creation of the world, the conception, death, and resurrection of Jesus Christ, or the regeneration of the fallen sinner, it is the Holy Spirit who is the power of God in action.

4. *He participates in divine authority*: The Holy Spirit occupies a place that is coequal with the Father and the Son in the statements in Scripture concerning the Trinity. In giving His final commission to the disciples immediately prior to His ascension to the Father, Jesus said, "Go and make disciples of all nations, baptizing them in the name of the Father and of the Son and of the Holy Spirit" (Matt. 28:19). All three members of the Trinity are behind the program to evangelize the world, and they operate together in unity. In his closing greeting at the end of his second letter to the Corinthians, Paul writes, "May the grace of the Lord Jesus Christ, and the love of God, and the fellowship of the Holy Spirit be with you all" (2 Cor. 13:14). The Holy Spirit is given equal status with the Father and the Son, acknowledging His identity as God.

The fact of the Trinity provides us with something of a mystery. There are three separate Beings with different identities and different roles. They are all God, but there is only one God. Yet the Father is not the Son, the Son is not the Spirit, and the Spirit is not the Father, although they are all the One God. The fact that this exceeds our understanding should not bother us unduly. If God is God we would expect aspects of His being and methods of His working to be outside of our limited understanding. If God could be fitted into our understanding, He would not be a very big God. We recognize God is infinite in His *existence*, for He had no beginning and will have no end. That defies our understanding. We acknowledge God is infinite in His *working*, for He created something out of nothing. That too defies our understanding. We must equally accept that God is infinite in His *person*. There is a complexity to God's being that is not paralleled in any part of creation, there is nothing in nature that might accurately illustrate the Trinity for us, and therefore we know only that which has been revealed, and what lies beyond revelation is, for the time being, a mystery. The book of Deuteronomy states, "The secret things belong to the Lord our God, but the things revealed belong to us and to our children forever" (Deut. 29:29). We can only speculate about the "secret things," and even that is unwise, but we must concern ourselves with the "things revealed." For the purpose of this study, the thing revealed is the deity of the Holy Spirit, coequal with the Father and the Son.

THE HOLY SPIRIT AND CHRIST

The relationship between the work of the Holy Spirit and the work of Christ is important. John records Jesus saying to His disciples, "I will ask the Father, and he will give you another Counselor to be with you forever—the Spirit of truth" (John 14:16–17). The Greek word which has been translated here as "another" is a significant one. It is the word *allos* which means "another of the same sort." The alternative word for "another" is *heteros* which means "another of a different sort." If you had a teaspoon in your hand and asked someone to bring you another spoon, by using the word *heteros*, they might bring you a tablespoon or a wooden spoon. It is another spoon but of a different kind. However, if you used the word *allos*, you would be asking for a spoon identical to the one you already hold, and you would be brought a teaspoon. The Holy Spirit's identity and ministry is the same as that of Jesus Christ. There is no discrepancy, conflict, or dispute of any kind between the work of Christ and the work of the Spirit.

Scripture sometimes interchanges expressions that speak of "Christ in us" and the "Spirit in us." This is not to create confusion or to indicate a dual presence in the life of a Christian, with Christ and the Spirit maintaining separate identities and fulfilling separate roles. It is the Holy Spirit who lives the life of Jesus Christ within us and who desires to express the character of Jesus Christ through us. The Spirit's presence and working is entirely Christ-centered and Christ-related.

The Spirit's teaching will not be original, but it will be the truth of Christ. Jesus stated, "But when he, the Spirit of truth, comes, he will guide you into all truth. He will not speak on his own; he will speak only what he hears, and he will tell you what is yet to come. He will bring glory to me by taking from what is mine and making it known to you" (John 16:13–14). His work will make us Christ-conscious, and the evidence of the Spirit's work is not to be found in a consciousness of the Spirit so much as in a consciousness of Christ. This may be one reason why the Holy Spirit is anonymous in Scripture as far as His personal name is concerned. We know Him by His title, but not by any name. It is because His purpose is to exalt Christ and to make us Christ-conscious and to lead us to live Christ-centered lives, not Spirit-centered lives. This is not to detract in any way from the dignity or deity of the Spirit, but to recognize His work.

Within the Trinity it is the Son who leads us to the Father. Jesus said, "I am the way and the truth and the life. No one comes to the Father except through me" (John 14:6), but it is the Spirit who enables us to know the Son; "No one can say 'Jesus is Lord,' except by the Holy Spirit" (1 Cor. 12:3). The Holy Spirit reveals Christ to us, and it is in knowing Christ that we come to the Father and are able to enjoy Him.

The reality of one's spiritual life will be found in one's knowledge of Christ, and the evidence of one's spiritual life will be found in one's likeness to Christ. We must be very careful of a Christianity which is centered on the Spirit's power, but which is detached from Christ's character. The Holy Spirit creates the character of Christ within us, as we shall see in the next chapter, so that people in our company are made conscious of Him.

I heard a story about a man who went overseas for a few years, leaving behind a girlfriend to whom he promised to write every day, and he did so faithfully. Day after day he put a letter in the post, and day after day she received one. When he eventually returned home, he discovered the girl had married the letter carrier! When the Lord Jesus Christ left earth, He promised the Holy Spirit, who would "bring glory to me." Do not marry the letter carrier, but allow the Holy Spirit, the revealer of Jesus Christ, to create a deep love for Him in your heart and an expression of His beauty in your character.

8

Marks of the Holy Spirit

How do you know when the Holy Spirit is living within you? It is very clear that we ought to know. After all, if He is God, and we claim that He comes to live within the lives of those who have faced their sin and repented of it, there ought to be some evidence that He is there. He does not come to hibernate, but to live and to work. What we believe about the Holy Spirit is only of value if it becomes expressed in our experience. We must recognize and believe the truths about the Holy Spirit as they are revealed in Scripture, but that is not enough. The truth has to step out of the Bible and into experience. I may hold in my hand a copy of a bus schedule that tells me the times of buses to a town I want to visit. The schedule may be true and accurate, but it will not get me to the town! The schedule is true, and it is important that I get my information from it, but only as I get onto the bus at a time I learn from the schedule and then ride into town so that the truth of the schedule has become my experience will the schedule have been of any value. It is sad that for so many in the church of Jesus Christ orthodoxy is measured in terms of *believing* the truth, rather than in terms of *experiencing* the truth. I am not calling for an experience-based Christianity. We must be wholly and firmly based on the objective revelation of Scripture, from which we must detract nothing and to which we must add nothing. However, we do need an experientially expressed Christianity, where the truths of the Bible become translated into experience and are seen to actually work in life.

When the apostle Paul came to Ephesus on his third missionary journey, he met some people described as being "disciples" and he asked them an interesting question, "Did you receive the Holy Spirit when you believed?" (Acts 19:2). Do not look for a subtle meaning in the question, it was a very straightforward one. He was asking,

"Are you Christians?" Had he asked them in that form, they might well have answered positively on the basis of a poor understanding of what it means to be a Christian. But the question he did ask could not be so easily evaded. He did not ask them a doctrinal question, but a question about their personal experience. Was there any evidence that the Holy Spirit had come to live within them? He expected them to know on the basis of their experience. Paul later wrote to the Romans, "The Spirit himself testifies with our spirit that we are God's children" (Rom. 8:16). There should not just be the objective testimony of Scripture that we are born again, but also the subjective testimony of the presence of the Spirit in our daily experience. John wrote, "And this is how we know that he lives in us: we know it by the Spirit he gave us" (1 John 3:24). Later he wrote, "We know that we live in him and he in us, because he has given us of his Spirit" (1 John 4:13). He says that we know we are Christians because we know the Holy Spirit is within us. I have heard it said on a number of occasions that if you are a Christian, you must have the Holy Spirit within you. That is a true statement in one sense, but I think the New Testament reverses the order. If you have the Holy Spirit, you must be a Christian. It is not being a Christian that gives you the right to have the Holy Spirit; it is having the Holy Spirit within that gives you the right to be a Christian.

You may think this is playing with words, but it is important. Paul told the Corinthians to "examine yourselves to see whether you are in the faith; test yourselves. Do you not realize that Jesus Christ is in you—unless, of course, you fail the test" (2 Cor. 13:5). He did not say, "Examine your Bibles to see whether you are in the faith," but "examine yourselves." I am fully aware that they didn't have Bibles at that stage, but the principle is the same, that we ought to expect evidence of the presence of the Holy Spirit in our lives.

What should we expect as the test of the Holy Spirit's presence? I am going to suggest three things, and I believe that the whole range of the Spirit's working will be found within these areas. This is by no means a full study of the work of the Holy Spirit within us, but these are the key features we would expect to find in a person in whom the Holy Spirit is being given the freedom to operate.

A HUNGER TO KNOW JESUS CHRIST

The first evidence of the Spirit's presence will be a new hunger to know Jesus Christ. We have already commented in the previous chapter on the fact that the Holy Spirit does not exalt or glorify Himself, but He does exalt and glorify Christ. It is the Spirit's task to reveal Christ (1 Cor. 12:3), to remind us of everything Christ has said (John 14:26), to testify about Christ (John 15:26), to bring glory to Christ (John 16:14), and to take of that which is Christ's and make it known to us (John 16:15).

One of the first evidences therefore that the Holy Spirit is working in someone's life is that Jesus Christ begins to be seen as attractive. He ceases to be detached and mystical but becomes real. It is the Holy Spirit who makes that happen. As I write this, my wife and I have been watching an entirely new attitude to Jesus Christ develop in the life of someone we know well, as the Holy Spirit has been drawing her to Christ. We believe she will soon come into a personal and living relationship with Christ, but her changed attitude to Him has been the mark of an authentic work of the Spirit so far.

Why is it that there is embarrassment about Jesus Christ among many who would claim to be Christian? They will talk about church and about meetings and even about the finer points of Christian doctrine, but are uncomfortable when talking about Christ. Very recently I was in the south of England for a series of meetings in a church. A family brought an eighteen-year-old girl who was living with them for a time, and who had never been exposed to the Gospel in this way before. God began to work in her life, and she borrowed a Bible and spent the whole of one day reading from it. At the meetings we held she drank in everything that was said, but found it difficult to understand why no one seemed to want to talk about Christ after the service was over. People stayed for coffee and talked about the weather, their holidays, or that "it was nice to see such a good number at the meeting," but no one seemed to want to talk about Christ! There are some super people in that church, many of them very godly, and this young woman's comment was a generalization perhaps, yet this is so often true. When there is not a hunger for Christ and a longing to know Him better and deeper, the Spirit of God is either absent or He is being quenched and grieved. We have pointed out already that the Christian life is a relationship, not just an experience or feelings. It is not just knowing *what* we believe, but in the words of Paul, "I know *whom* I have believed," and it is to know Him better that is an expression of the Spirit's life within us.

One of the first signs that people are in love is that they have a tremendous desire to get to know each other better. Each will gladly talk about the other, listen to others talk about him or her, and above all will spend as much time as possible in the other's company. It is true that there may be barriers of shyness and inhibitions that prevent them being as open as they would like to be and which will hopefully be overcome, but there is a great desire to know the loved one better.

Is there a hunger deep within you to know and love the Lord Jesus Christ better? Perhaps there are fears about expressing that in some ways, but if the desire is there it is one evidence of the Spirit within you.

One of the ways our desire to know Christ will express itself is in a new appetite for the Bible. The Bible supremely is a revelation of Christ. Jesus once talked to some Jews about the futility of Bible study. He said, "You diligently study the Scriptures because you think that by them you possess eternal life. These are the Scriptures that testify about me, yet you refuse to come to me to have life" (John 5:39–40). They studied the Scriptures because they wanted to know the Scriptures, and it did them no good whatsoever! Jesus told them that the purpose of studying the Scriptures is to discover Christ, for the Scriptures are a revelation of Him. This is why it is good to read the Bible daily—not as some kind of fetish, so that if you miss your Bible reading you are likely to be knocked down by a bus, but because it reveals Christ and there is a hunger in your heart to know Him more. This is why, if Christ is not real to a person, the Bible is such a boring book! The Bible only makes sense in the light of Jesus Christ. When people come to know Christ, they discover the Bible to be a new book.

I travel away from home much of my time, and this often involves overseas trips that may last several weeks or months. At such times, the mail becomes very important to me, and I love getting letters from my wife. I always enjoy reading her letters (it is one of the perks of being away from home) and will go through them several times. But if I was to offer them to someone else to read, he or she would probably find them extremely tedious. Someone may, out of politeness to me, read them through once, but it is highly unlikely anyone would want to read them again or make a photocopy! The reason is very simple. The writer is someone I know and love and care for, and what concerns her concerns me. I am interested in the family, the weather, the things that have gone wrong, and the things that have gone right. The letter itself is valuable to me because it is a revelation of the person. So it is with Scripture. A love for the Lord Jesus Christ will always take you to His Word, so that through the written Word, there might be a revelation of the Living Word, the Lord Jesus Himself. I am extremely concerned about those who claim a working of the Holy Spirit that has cut into their appetite for the Bible. It is suspect, because the work of the Spirit is to bring us ever closer to Christ and therefore takes us to His Word.

A HUNGER TO BE LIKE JESUS CHRIST

Not only will we find a hunger to know Christ, but a hunger to be like Christ. Paul talks about those things which will be the "fruit of the Spirit" in the lives of Christians. By "fruit" he is describing the inevitable consequences of the Spirit's presence in their lives. "The fruit of the Spirit is love, joy, peace, patience, kindness, goodness, faithfulness, gentleness, and self-control" (Gal. 5:22–23). You will notice that the list is in the singular, "the fruit of the Spirit is," and not "the fruits of the Spirit are." These are not nine different fruits, some of which may be evidenced in one life and others in another, but all nine qualities are together the expression of the Spirit's work in our lives. One word sums up this list: *character*. More specifically, it is the character of Jesus Christ, because the Spirit who produced this so perfectly in His life is the one who wants to express the same qualities in our lives. The Devil can counterfeit the gifts of the Spirit (the purpose for which they are given we will comment on later), but he cannot counterfeit the fruit of the Spirit for it is an expression of the very character of God, and he hates that!

This changed character will be expressed in three ways: a changed attitude to people; a changed attitude to circumstances; a changed attitude to ourselves.

A changed attitude to people: The first word on the list of fruit is *love*, and it is followed later by "kindness, goodness, faithfulness," and "gentleness," all of which are expressions of love and which are seen in our attitude toward other people.

Love was spoken of by Jesus as the evidence of being a Christian when He said, "All men will know that you are my disciples if you love one another" (John 13:35). The reason for this is clear: "God is love" (1 John 2:5), and the evidence of love is an indication of the restoration of the character of God. We have seen in an earlier chapter that to be restored to His likeness is the object of salvation.

There are two words for "love" in the New Testament, and the one used here is *agape*. It is not so much *emotional* as it is *volitional*, that is, it is not just a feeling toward someone but an attitude of mind and will toward him or her. It is best expressed in Paul's letter to the Philippians in which he writes, "Do nothing out of selfish ambition or vain conceit, but in humility consider others better than yourselves. Each of you should look not only to your own interests, but also to the interests of others" (Phil. 2:3–4). The wording, "consider others better than yourselves," may sound as though it involves a value judgment that considers oneself to be not as good as others, but the New American Standard Version translates it helpfully: "But with humility of mind let each of you regard one another as more important than himself." That is the essence of *agape* love, considering others as "more important" than yourself. One of the evidences that you are loved by someone is that you begin to feel important to that one. With the Holy Spirit at work in our lives, people become important, and there is a new attitude toward them in general.

Love is more than a feeling toward people we like. It is an attitude, even toward those we might not like or get on with naturally, which says, "They are more important to me than I am to myself in the moments that I am involved with them." Let us be realistic about this. Most people manage to get along with people they like without the aid of the Holy Spirit, but the love of God working through a person is going to be much deeper than that.

On one occasion I was leading a two-week conference in Austria in which we had a number of folks from Great Britain. One of the people in the group was telling me about the tremendous work God had been doing among the young people in his church fellowship, and particularly how they had been bound together with a real love for one another. It sounded good, and I asked him one morning to take a few minutes in one of the teaching sessions and share some of their experience with the whole group, as I thought this would be encouraging to us all. However, while he was speaking, I noticed that he only mentioned the young people in the church and said nothing about any older ones. Later that day I asked him if there were any older people in the church. He began to smile and said, "Oh, that is a different story. The young people and the older people don't get on in our church, so apart from Sunday morning, we meet separately for all the other meetings." I said to him that although he had told us in his talk that the Holy Spirit had given the young people such a great love for each other, it was probably a mistake to attribute it to the Holy Spirit. It does not take the Spirit of God to get a group of young people with similar outlook, similar background, and similar experience to develop a love for each other. That will happen naturally. Neither does it take the Holy Spirit to cause the older folks in the church to gang together and find it more comfortable to meet separately from the young people because they do not understand them fully. When the Holy Spirit is the source of love you will find the older people saying that, although they may not understand the young people or feel especially comfortable with them, they regard them as being more important to them than their own comforts are to themselves. They will want to build them up and serve them. Similarly, the young people will say of the older people that, although they don't particularly enjoy their outlook on things, they love them, and they are more important to them than their own freedoms, and they want to encourage them, learn from them, and build them up too.

To love only those who love us is described by Jesus as "pagan love." "If you love those who love you, what reward will you get? Are not even the tax collectors doing that? And if you greet only your brothers, what are you doing more than others? Do not even pagans do that?" (Matt. 5:46–47). The kind of love this man described as being among the young people in his church seemed to be little different to the kind of love you might find in the public house around the corner where the criterion for meeting was that everyone liked each other's company, and those that didn't get on went elsewhere!

The love of God in our lives is not a love that reinforces the natural divisions among people by only making the love we already have for certain people stronger, but it is a love that breaks down the natural barriers. Please do not misunderstand me. I am not saying that love causes us to avoid differences, but it is in the context of love that we are to face and deal with them. Where there are real differences between people, to love at the expense of truth and conviction would not be a real love. If we bury major differences in the interests of what we may feel to be love, these differences will emerge again. In a loving context we should face difficulties honestly and securely, and there may even be times when separation is inevitable as a result, such as a case like the disagreement between Paul and Barnabas, recorded in Acts 15, which was so sharp that the best solution was to part company. But even in the context of disagreement and separation on the grounds of different ideas or principles, the other must remain the object of our love, being more important to us than we are to ourselves. That will take the Holy Spirit, and that is what He wants to produce.

The classic description of love in Scripture is in Paul's first letter to the Corinthians, chapter 13, part of which says, "love is patient, love is kind. It does not envy, it does not boast, it is not proud. It is not rude, it is not self-seeking, it is not easily angered, it keeps no record of wrongs. Love does not delight in evil but rejoices with the truth. It always protects, always trusts, always hopes, always perseveres. Love never fails" (1 Cor. 13:4–8). If you were to read that again and replace the word *love* with *Christ*, it would make perfect sense. Jesus Christ was the incarnation of love, for God is love. But this too is the goal of the Holy Spirit in your life and mine. It may be a challenging and humbling process, but read through these same verses some time and instead of "love" read your own name. The extent of our embarrassment reveals how far we have to grow, as well as how honest we are. In this life we will not be perfect, although the day will come when we shall be perfectly restored to the likeness of Christ. In the meantime, this is our goal, and the appetite to be like Christ is the effect of the Holy Spirit's presence and working within us.

In the list Paul gives to the Galatian Christians of the fruit of the Spirit, our attitude to people will also find its expression in *kindness, goodness, faithfulness,* and *gentleness.* These are very practical expressions of our love and care for others.

The appetite to be like Jesus is not expressed in a pious, smug feeling, where we sit in a corner detached from a dirty world making sure our halos remain pure, but it is seeing people as more important than ourselves, both inside and outside the church, and being prepared to get our hands dirty in their interests.

A changed attitude to circumstances: Several other qualities Paul lists among the fruit of the Spirit are "joy," "peace," and "patience." Each of us is vulnerable to difficult circumstances that rob us of our joy, disturb our peace, and exhaust our patience. The Holy Spirit brings a whole new attitude and perspective on our problems.

A Christian is not exempt from difficulties, as some would assume, but rather he is equipped to go into them and to survive.

Joy is something different from happiness. Happiness is a comfortable feeling determined by circumstances. If you are lying on a beach on a hot day with a big ice cream in one hand and someone you love beside you, you might well be described as being happy. But if a black cloud comes between you and the sun and then begins to drop large cold raindrops on you, your loved one gets up and walks away, the ice cream falls into the sand, and the tide comes in and washes away your clothes, you might well lose your sense of happiness! It has been related to nice circumstances, and it is superficial. Joy, however, is something far deeper. It is a confidence in God that sees beyond the circumstances. When Paul wrote to the Philippians, he was a prisoner in Rome. He describes himself as being in chains; he tells of people who are trying to make trouble for him while he is there; he admits to being in tears as he writes about the enemies of the Cross of Christ; yet in the same letter he writes, "Rejoice in the Lord always. I will say it again: Rejoice" (Phil. 4:4). Paul did not say this because he enjoyed his suffering, but because he could see beyond his hardships and was able to rejoice in the goodness of God and the working of God. In Nehemiah's day, even when things have been hard, Nehemiah was able to say, "The joy of the Lord is your strength" (Neh. 8:10).

Peace is something different from tranquillity. On one occasion a painting competition was held, and the theme of each picture was to be "peace." There were two prize winners. One had gone to the Lake District in the northwest of England and painted a beautiful landscape with a calm lake in the foreground, and hills in the background covered in well-ordered coniferous trees that extended down to the water's edge, casting an almost mirror reflection into the lake. There were just one or two little puffs of white cloud in the sky, and in the foreground on the lake a duck and her few ducklings were gently floating by in the warmth of the sunshine and tranquillity of the setting. The painting won second prize.

The other artist had gone to Cornwall and had painted a picture of a thunder storm. On the left of the picture was a rugged cliff that plunged into the sea and the waves were lashing violently against the rocks. On top of the cliff was a tree at almost a forty-five degree angle as a strong gale blew in from the sea. The sky was covered with black cloud, the rain was hard and harsh, and a flash of lightning occupied the top right hand side of the painting. About two thirds of the way up the cliff there was a cleft in the rock; in the cleft there was a nest, and on the nest there sat a gull with its eyes closed. The artist called his painting "Peace" and won first prize!

The peace of God does not mean our removal from difficulties but is to be our experience within them, like the Lord Jesus Christ asleep on a cushion in the boat with His disciples when a "furious storm came up on the lake, so that the waves swept over the boat" (Matt. 8:24). That was some storm! The waves were coming right over the boat. Everyone else was in a panic, but the Lord Jesus was asleep. His disciples soon woke Him and rebuked Him for His irresponsibility! He knew He was in bigger hands than the elements of nature and accordingly rebuked the disciples for their lack of faith.

Paul told the Philippians, "Do not be anxious about anything, but in everything, by prayer and petition, with thanksgiving, present your requests to God. And the peace of God, which transcends all understanding, will guard your hearts and your minds in Christ Jesus" (Phil. 4:6–7). He acknowledges there will be situations in which we would normally be anxious, but instead of being anxious, present the situation to God and leave it with Him. If you can trust Him, you will not need to worry any more, because He will take care of the situation. He won't worry about our problems either, for He doesn't even worry about His own. So instead of panic, there is peace, and it is a "peace which transcends all understanding," which means you may not be able to explain it to people who think you ought to be a little more troubled about the problem than you are. God does not invite us to escape from our problems but to prove His sufficiency within them.

Patience is very much related to peace. Our peace is threatened when we are concerned about what is happening to us now. When we are beyond and are able to look back, we can see things in a different light. It is patience that helps us to see beyond the present and to wait. Interestingly, it is difficulties that teach us to be patient. Paul wrote, "Tribulation worketh patience" (Rom. 5:3, AV). A well-known preacher was once asked by a woman if he would pray for her as she had a great need for patience, which she seemed to have only in short supply. He agreed to do so, and as they knelt to pray he began to ask the Lord to bring tough times into her life and to take her through such tribulation as she had never experienced before. Before he could finish the woman jumped to her feet, grabbed him by the shoulders, and said, "Stop! I have enough of that already." He explained to her that "tribulation worketh patience," and it would only be out of her troubles that she would discover patience. Very often our troubles are our kindest friends because of what they teach us and do for us.

The presence of the Holy Spirit in our lives will be expressed in new attitudes to circumstances, and we will be characterized by joy, peace, and patience.

A changed attitude to ourselves: The fruit of the Spirit's presence will be seen in "self-control." The Bible does not talk about coming under Spirit-control, but rather that the Spirit will bring us under self-control. Talk of being controlled by the Spirit has evolved over the years but is not, strictly speaking, a biblical idea. The NIV does translate the expression *in the Spirit* to being "controlled by the Spirit" in one or two places, but this would seem to me to be unwise. The Spirit will not control us in the sense that He makes us do things, but He will enable us to control ourselves. There are many things that threaten to control us—our habits, greed, selfishness, and pride, but the Spirit enables us to have ourselves under control so that instead of doing what we are driven to do, we act under control. This, of course, is true freedom. Solomon wrote, "Like a city whose walls are broken down is a man who lacks self-control" (Prov. 25:28).

None of these things is automatic to us. They have to be worked on. The Holy Spirit creates the desire and gives enabling, but this does not exclude our need for discipline in all of the areas covered by the fruit of the Spirit. Peter wrote, "His divine power has given us everything we need for life and godliness through our knowledge of him who called us by his own glory and goodness. . . . For this very reason, make every effort to add to your faith goodness . . . knowledge . . . self-control . . . perseverance . . . godliness . . . brotherly kindness . . . love" (2 Peter 1:3–7). On the basis of all that we have in Christ which is sufficient for our lives and godliness, Peter says we have to "make every effort" to bring these qualities increasingly into experience.

Part of the work of the Holy Spirit, therefore, is to create in us a hunger to be like Jesus Christ, so that the qualities that made the life of Christ so attractive to people and so pleasing to God will increasingly be exhibited in our lives.

But just one last word about this. We have been looking at the *fruit* of the Spirit, not the *flowers* of the Spirit! There is a difference between flowers and fruit. Flowers are decorative. They are nice to look at and having them around makes the atmosphere pleasant. But fruit is for consumption! It is there to be eaten by hungry people. We are not talking about qualities that make Christians nice to look at, but about qualities that enable them to meet the needs of others. We are going to meet people who are hungry for love, and they will have the right to eat the fruit of our love. There will be people who are hungry for joy, peace, and patience, and who will benefit from those qualities in our lives. There are those who may need to lean upon our stability as those under self-control, when they themselves are discouraged and plagued with things out of control in their lives. The Holy Spirit will bear fruit in our lives so that other people may come and eat the fruit. Are you prepared for that? It is all to do with being equipped to serve, which brings us to the third test of the Holy Spirit's working in our lives.

He not only creates a hunger to know Jesus Christ and a hunger to be like Jesus Christ, but:

A HUNGER TO SERVE JESUS CHRIST

The Holy Spirit comes *to* us that He might flow *through* us. Jesus stood up on the last day of the Feast of Tabernacles in Jerusalem on one occasion and said, "If a man is thirsty, let him come to me and drink. Whoever believes in me, as the Scripture has said, streams of living water will flow from within him," and John adds the explanation, "By this he meant the Spirit, whom those who believed in him were later to receive" (John 7:37–39). The Spirit is described by Jesus as being like a stream of living water that will flow from within the believer. The Spirit is not poured into lives like water poured into a cup but like water poured into a pipe. When a cup is full, it is full! But everything that is poured into a pipe will flow through it. That is the picture of our lives. A mark of the Spirit's presence is a hunger for God to flow through us in blessing and enrichment to others. Looking after ourselves first has nothing to do with the Christian life and nothing to do with the work of the Holy Spirit.

When Jesus promised power to His disciples, on the day that the Holy Spirit would be given soon after His ascension, it was power to witness. "You will receive power when the Holy Spirit comes on you; and you will be my witnesses in Jerusalem, in all Judea, in Samaria, and to the ends of the earth" (Acts 1:8). The promise was not to make people powerful for their own sakes, but to equip them to serve God and fulfill His plans by bearing witness to the Lord Jesus Christ throughout the world. If the Spirit of God is within your life, then you will find a new desire to serve, unless, of course, you are quenching the Spirit.

It is for this reason that the New Testament speaks of spiritual gifts being given to the church. A total of twenty-two different abilities are described as "gifts" in the New Testament. The list is not intended to be exhaustive, for the most mentioned to any single church was eleven, exactly half of all that are mentioned, and these are in the first letter to the Corinthians. There are other abilities we should equally recognize as spiritual gifts that do not get a mention at all. There is no mention in the New Testament of anyone having the gift of singing or of hymn writing or of counseling, but we recognize these to be valuable to the upbuilding and growth of the church. It is not relevant to discuss the content of spiritual gifts here, rather, their purpose. They are given as tools to equip us to serve the Lord Jesus Christ effectively.

Peter wrote, "Each one should use whatever gift he has received to serve others, faithfully administering God's grace in its various forms" (1 Peter 4:10). Paul wrote, "Now to each one the manifestation of the Spirit is given for the common good" (1 Cor. 12:7). These are never given for self-gratification or for personal use, but for the upbuilding of the church of Jesus Christ.

In the light of that, I believe it is a mistake to be gift-centered. We need rather to be service-centered. I do not feel it is appropriate to ask someone, "What is your spiritual gift?" but we should be asking, "What are you doing to serve the Lord Jesus Christ?" To this day I have never tried to analyze what my gift or gifts might be; I simply try to serve effectively wherever I can and do what God gives me to do. I believe it is in this way we discover practically how to be useful and where our gifts and abilities may lie. I do not feel comfortable when people ask me how they can find their gifts. I would far rather hear someone ask where and how they could be involved in service for the Lord Jesus Christ, for as we get busy we soon discover where our abilities are and where they are not.

Just imagine you were part of a team of people who were going to spring-clean a house. At the beginning of the day, the person in charge may say something like, "There are a dozen of us here to do this job, and there are certain tools available to help us to do it effectively. We have two vacuum cleaners, one broom, one mop, two paint brushes, two cans of polish, one window cleaner, and three damp cloths. Now each of you desire to get hold of one of these and get on with the job." This seems to be the thinking behind Paul's urging of the Corinthian Christians to "eagerly desire spiritual gifts" (1 Cor. 14:1). He is saying that there is a job to be done, God has equipped us with various abilities to accomplish it, so we should eagerly desire to be involved in God's program and get on with the job. Although activities differ, there is a job in the service of Jesus Christ for everyone. The two who get hold of the vacuum cleaners in the house are not more important than those who get hold of the three damp cloths; they are all fulfilling different functions to complete the same job. God has things for you to do, which is a privilege. The Holy Spirit's presence within your life will be evidenced by a desire to serve Him and a discovering of His enabling to do so.

We could say a lot more about this, but our purpose is to speak of the marks of the Holy Spirit being active and free within our lives. Is there an appetite in your heart to serve the Lord Jesus Christ and to accomplish the things that please Him, even if few others recognize your role?

Many things are included in the work of the Spirit, but as His work is Christ-centered, they will come into the orbit of these three areas. There will be a hunger to know Jesus Christ, a hunger to be like Jesus Christ, and a hunger to serve Jesus Christ, with all the attending means of doing so.

In conclusion, I have chosen to use the word *hunger* to describe our attitude to these things very carefully. To hunger for something is to be needing it and wanting it. Hunger is not a satisfied feeling, but a yearning for something. Jesus used this word when He said, "Blessed are they who hunger and thirst for righteousness" (Matt. 5:6). The truth is not that we have arrived at any of these things, but that we have an appetite to do so. Jesus did not say, "Blessed are those who are righteous" but blessed are those who "hunger and thirst for righteousness." He did promise that they would be satisfied, and we anticipate that as we allow the Holy Spirit to take us deeper and deeper into the person and concerns of Jesus Christ, there will be a growing satisfaction with all that we find Him to be and with all that He gives us to do. This is the evidence of the Holy Spirit within us.

9

Living by Faith

If we were to construct a top ten list of the most misunderstood words in the Christian vocabulary, I would nominate the word *faith* for the number one spot. It is a word which introduces us to a key factor in Christian living, designed to bring freedom, liberty, and power into our experience. Yet, like no other word, it has brought frustration, discouragement, and even a sense of condemnation to people.

It is by faith that truth becomes experience, and without it truth remains elusive, impractical, and theoretical. The writer of the book of Hebrews, comparing Israel in the Old Testament to his readers, states, "For we also have had the gospel preached to us, just as they did; but the message they heard was of no value to them, because those who heard it did not combine it with faith" (Heb. 4:2). Two groups of people heard the same truth. To the one it was of immense value, but to the other it was of no value at all. The reason? One group combined what they knew with faith, and the other did not. It was the combination of truth with faith that made the truth work and become effective in their lives.

One thing we cannot escape as we read the Bible is that faith is an indispensable part of Christian experience. The Scripture tells us that we are cleansed by faith, that we are saved by faith, that we are justified by faith, and that we have access to God by faith. However, having been saved by faith, we also discover that we are to live by faith, to walk by faith, and in so doing we discover we are to fight the good fight of faith, to take the shield of faith, and to overcome the world by faith. We then discover that without faith it is impossible to please Him, and that whatever is not of faith is sin. Therefore, whatever else we may think about faith, we have to agree it is important! Furthermore, if we have difficulty living the Christian life, in all probability our difficulty will be related to our exercise of faith or our lack of it.

WHAT IS FAITH?

The first thing we must do is define the word. Undefined words can be a source of much confusion, especially when one person listening to a word has a different understanding than the person using it. That is bound to be confusing! Before defining faith positively, allow me to comment on two popular, but mistaken, ideas as to the meaning of faith.

1. *Faith in not a mystical power.* Some think of faith as a force, a mind-over-matter phenomenon whereby the actual act of believing something has the effect of making it come true. Somebody once rebuked me for saying it was going to be a miserable day when I should, I was told, have said it was going to be a beautiful day. The facts were that, although it was midsummer in the north of England, it had been raining all the previous night, the clouds were heavy and still raining, and the forecast was that there would be no change. Being realistic about these facts, I commented to the effect that things did not look as though they would improve and that it was going to be a "miserable day." After the rebuke and instruction that I should have said it was going to be "beautiful," I made it worse by insisting, "But it is not. It is cold, it is wet, and it is forecast to stay that way all day." "But," I was rebuked, "you should say it is going to be beautiful." "Why?" I asked, and received the reply, "That is faith. If you believe it will be a fine day, it will become a fine day." Now that is not faith. It may be wishful thinking, but it is much nearer to foolishness than to faith! If the facts are that it is wet and cold, no matter how much I might "believe" in sunshine, it will remain wet and cold. Believing something never, in itself, changes the facts. Faith is not a mystical power that makes things happen by the sheer force of belief.

2. *Faith is not a substitute for facts.* Some see faith as something which comes into play only when we run out of facts! As long as we have facts we are secure, but when facts run out or things become a little uncertain, it is then we need to exercise faith. In other words, a basic ingredient in the exercise of faith is a good imagination—a willingness to believe in things that cannot be substantiated.

It is the reverse of this which is actually true. Faith is not an alternative to facts, but faith is valid only when it is placed in facts. Faith must be placed in something. Faith does not exist in itself, but only as an attitude toward an object. In this respect it is like love. Love does not exist other than in an attitude toward something or someone. Just imagine meeting a girl who appeared weak at the knees, whose eyes were rolling, and who was clearly a little giddy. You ask her what is the matter and she replies, "I am in love." "With whom?" you ask. "Oh, no one," she replies, "I am just in love." That would not be possible, and it would not be love! Love is not just a feeling one gets in isolation, but an attitude toward someone (or something).

Similarly with faith. Faith is not shutting your eyes, clenching your fist, and believing something into being, but rather it is an attitude of trust toward something which enables that something to function in response. If I place faith in my car, it means that I adopt an attitude of trust toward the car that enables it to take me along the road. The car does the work, and it is my willingness to get into the car and allow it to transport me that is the exercise of faith. It is the object in which we place our faith that determines whether the faith is effective or not. If I place a lot of faith in a weak chair and decide to sit on it, I will very soon find myself in a crumpled heap on the floor. My problem was not lack of faith, but the weakness of the object in which I placed my faith. All the faith in the world will not make up for weakness in the object in which my faith has been placed. Conversely, a little faith will not detract from the ability of a strong object. If I place a little faith in some thick ice and very nervously step on to the ice with an inflated ring around my waist, holding on to a rope that is tied to the nearest tree, and having made sure my last will and testament is in order, I will discover that I am able to walk on top of the ice! This is not because I had a lot of faith, but because the object in which I have placed my faith is strong. The most important thing about faith is not the faith, but the object in which we are prepared to place our faith, for faith is allowing that object to act on our behalf.

In the Christian life, the object of our faith is the Lord Jesus Christ. The exercise of faith is an attitude of trust toward Him which enables Him to be what He is and to do what He does within our own experience. When Scripture states that we are "saved by faith," it means that we recognize our utter inability to save ourselves, and in dependence upon Christ we say something like, "Lord Jesus, I cannot save myself, but You can save me. I trust You to do so." The result of our faith in Him is that *He* is able to work, for the result of exercising faith is that God is able to work for us, in us, and through us.

This is how the Christian life is designed to function. Many Christians recognize the need for Christ to save them, and the act of becoming a Christian by faith is a basic and fundamental idea to them. However, the problems come when there is a failure to recognize the equal necessity to live each day by faith in the same way that they became Christians by faith in the first place! It was this problem that provoked the apostle Paul to ask the Galatian Christians, in his letter to them, "Did you receive the Spirit by observing the law, or by believing what you heard?" (Gal. 3:2). Now that is a basic issue. Do we receive the Spirit on the basis of our works and our own abilities, or do we receive Him by faith? The answer is that we receive Him by faith. Paul then continues, "Are you so foolish? After beginning with the Spirit, are you now trying to attain your goal by human effort?" (Gal. 3:3). "You fools," Paul is saying, "you recognize your need to receive the Spirit by faith, but having done that you are trying to live the Christian life by your own ability, as though God was on the sidelines watching but not actually involved."

So serious was this error on their part that Paul describes them as having been "bewitched" (Gal. 3:1). One of the most important things to discover about the Christian life, and one of the things the Devil will seek to undermine more than anything else, is the indispensability of Jesus Christ Himself to its working. If the Christian life was nothing more than something we lived for God, it would be reduced to the ranks of just another religion and would be as dull and legalistic as the rest of them. The Christian life is not something we live for God, but something God lives in us. From start to finish it is a life of faith in God's ability to work.

I believe it is a great pity that the expression "living by faith" has become a technical term among many Christians, applying only to those who have been called by God to serve Him in a capacity where they have no fixed income and are wholly dependent upon God to meet their financial and physical needs. God does call many to that kind of circumstance, but to term this exclusively as "living by faith" is a misnomer. Every Christian is called to live by faith. It has little or nothing to do with where we get our money from, but has everything to do with our attitude to God. So vital is this that the alternative to living by faith is living in sin, for, "everything that does not come from faith is sin" (Rom. 14:23). Biblically speaking, when something is described as being a "faith work," it is simply being stated that it is not a "sin work." When people tell you they are "living by faith," they are saying that they are not "living in sin," which is always good to know, especially if they are in some kind of "full-time Christian work"! Living by faith is the basis upon which every Christian is called to live, because the only alternative to living in *dependence* upon God is to be acting in *independence* of God. It is the attitude of independence that is the essence of sin.

When speaking of the work of the Holy Spirit on one occasion, Jesus said, "When he comes, he will convict the world of guilt in regard to sin . . . in regard to sin, because men do not believe in me" (John 16:8–9). "Sin" is all that which does not derive from belief in Jesus Christ. In this context we need to define the word *belief* too, for there are two ways in which it can be used. If I were to ask you whether you believe in the Loch Ness monster or not, and then to ask you whether you believe in aspirin or not, I would be asking you two very different questions. When I ask if you believe in the Loch Ness monster I want to know if you believe that in Loch Ness in Scotland there lurks a monster with a long neck, a couple of humps, and which disappears whenever people go looking for it, reappearing only once in a while, and generally coinciding with the time the local taverns and bars close. Your response may be "Yes" or it may be "No." You either believe in its existence or you don't. Either way it is not terribly important, unless you happen to run a souvenir shop on the banks of Loch Ness. Belief in this respect is purely an intellectual exercise.

However, when I ask you if you believe in aspirin, I take for granted your awareness of the existence of aspirin as a source of pain relief, and my question has no relationship to whether you are intellectually aware of its existence or not. What I am asking is, "If you have a headache, do you take aspirin and allow it to work on your behalf?" Belief, in this sense, is being prepared to let what you know exists work.

This is the "belief" used of our relationship to Christ in the New Testament. It is not just a belief in His existence, but the kind of belief that lets Him work. Of course, we must exercise the first kind of belief, for "anyone who comes to him must believe that he exists" (Heb. 11:6), but that in itself doesn't do us any good. James writes, "You believe that there is one God. Good! Even the demons believe that—and shudder" (James 2:19). However, it is on the basis of the first kind of belief that we must *belief in God's existence and to the point of allowing Him to work through you.*

exercise the second kind of belief, which is an attitude toward Him that lets Him work.

It is this failure to believe, failure to let Him work, which is the essence of sin. When we are acting in independence of God, rather than in dependence upon God, even though the activity in itself may be good and legitimate, we are actually committing sin. It is not a case of failure to believe in Jesus Christ being the biggest sin, and hence Jesus' promise that the Holy Spirit would convict the world of sin "because they do not believe in me," but it is the fact that anything at all which does not derive from dependence upon God is sin. The thing that pleases God in our lives is the disposition toward Him that allows Him to be God and to work within us and through us. That is why, "without faith it is impossible to please him" (Heb. 11:6).

Living by faith, therefore, is holding a disposition toward Jesus Christ that recognizes His authority as Lord over me and His enabling as my life within me. It has less to do with the nature of our activities than it has to do with their cause. We will explore this further, but first a problem.

When talking about living by faith, one of the most frequent responses in people's minds is the feeling that they do not have enough faith. People have often said, "If only I had more faith," or have looked across to someone else and said, "I wish I had his [her] faith." Many of us have prayed the simple prayer, "Lord, increase my faith." If you have ever prayed that you are in good company for it is exactly the request the disciples of Jesus made to Him on one occasion. However, the response of the Lord probably surprised them as much as it may surprise you.

The incident is found in Luke 17:5–6: "The apostles said to the Lord, 'Increase our faith!' He replied, 'If you have faith as small as a mustard seed, you can say to this mulberry tree, "Be uprooted and planted in the sea," and it will obey you.'" Mustard seed was the smallest known seed in the Middle East at the time, so in response to the request for an increase in faith, Jesus used something very small to illustrate what was necessary. What did He mean? The point surely was this: If the most important thing about faith is the object in which it is placed, then the actual quantity of the faith is secondary. If you place a little faith in a strong object, the object will still function. In other words, the Lord was saying that in asking a question like that, the disciples were showing that they did not understand the nature of faith. The all-important thing is not the quantity of our faith, but the quality of the object in which our faith is placed. Small faith in a strong object will still enable that object to work.

MUSTARD, POTATO, AND WATERMELON

Let me illustrate this point. I well remember the first time I ever flew in an airplane. When I was growing up, I used to love watching aircraft and would dream about one day being able to fly in one. When I was eighteen I was given a job on a large farm in Zimbabwe in southern Africa (then known as Rhodesia). I remember going to Heathrow Airport in London in order to catch my flight, and I was partly excited, but at the same time partly frightened. I had heard all sorts of stories about planes crashing, and I feared it could well happen while I was on board! I went to the check-in counter and received my boarding pass with my seat assignment. The aircraft was a Boeing 707, with rows of three seats on either side of the isle. My seat was the middle of three on the left side of the aircraft. When I got there, an elderly woman was already sitting in the seat to my left, next to the window. As I sat down I noticed that she was rather agitated and, to say the least, very nervous. She was gripping the armrest so tightly that her knuckles were white! After a short while we began to talk. She asked me if I had ever flown before and told me, much as I had suspected, that she hadn't either. She explained to me that her daughter and son-in-law had emigrated to Rhodesia and now had three children whom she had never seen. They had sent her a round-trip plane ticket as a present, enabling her to go and visit them. She confided in me that "if it wasn't for my grandchildren, I would not risk my life like this." She really was afraid.

Soon after I had taken my seat, a South African businessman came and sat next to me. He had flown many times before, and having sat down, took out a book and began to read. He seemed oblivious to everything going on around him and certainly didn't express any concern or show any fear.

Presently we started to move toward the end of the runway and prepare for take-off. As the engines opened up, the woman next to me seemed to shrivel in fear. As the noise of the engines got louder she seemed to get smaller. Presently we began to move, and as we lifted off the ground her head was tucked into her lap, just waiting for something to go wrong! I was at the same time experiencing the combination of exhilaration on the one hand and fear on the other. The man on my right, in contrast to both of us, was completely relaxed and at ease. He just continued to read his book. It was a sixteen-hour journey to Zimbabwe with three stops enroute. During that time the woman began to relax just a little, I relaxed much, much more, and the man on my right was completely relaxed as he ate, read, drank, or slept.

The reason I tell you this is because the three of us in that row each had a different quantity of faith. The woman had only mustard-seed-sized faith. She had just enough to allow herself to be persuaded to make the journey, and when she added up the pros and cons she decided there was a fifty-one percent chance that she would survive. I, however, was a little more confident and had potato-sized faith. I was by no means confident that all would go well, but I seemed to know a little bit more about the track record of aircraft than she did and knew that the overwhelming likelihood was that we would survive and get to our destination in one piece. The man on my right probably never even thought about there being any possibility of his not arriving safely as he bounded on board with his mountain-sized faith. But the remarkable thing was this: Although the woman had only mustard-seed-sized faith and I had potato-sized faith and the man on my right had mountain-sized faith, we all arrived at our destination at the same time. The man with a lot of faith did not arrive first, with me coming in second, and the woman arriving about six hours behind me. The all-important thing was not the quantity of our faith but the object in which we placed our faith. Having placed our faith in the aircraft, whether mustard-seed-size, potato-size, or mountain-size, it was then the plane that did the work of getting us to our destination. If someone had asked me on arrival how I had traveled from London, I would not have replied, "By faith," though that would surely be a legitimate statement. I would reply, "By aircraft," for it was the object in which I placed my faith that actually did the work.

That is why in response to the request by the disciples for an increased faith, the effect of Jesus' reply was to say that the quantity of their faith was a secondary issue to the object of their faith. If they were to place the little faith they did have in God, they would see God work. On the few other occasions when Jesus rebuked the disciples for their "little faith," it was never a reference to little quantity but that their faith was of little duration. It hadn't lasted very long. For example, when Peter had been with the other disciples on the Sea of Galilee during a storm, Jesus came to them walking on the water. Peter had shouted, "Lord, if it is you, tell me to come to you on the water" (Matt. 14:28). Jesus had replied "Come," and Peter got out of the boat and found himself experiencing the same miracle as he too walked on the water and came to Jesus. We do not know how long or how far Peter walked, but after a while Matthew records, "When he saw the wind, he was afraid and, beginning to sink, cried out, 'Lord, save me!' Immediately Jesus reached out his hand and caught him. 'You of little faith,' he said, 'why did you doubt?'" (Matt. 14:30–31). Peter had trusted for a while, but when he began to look around and notice the wind and the circumstances he was in, he became afraid as the storm loomed larger in his reckoning than the power of the Lord Jesus Christ. As a result he began to sink, and he was rebuked for his little faith, not in the sense that he didn't have much, but that it didn't last long. He stopped trusting. It was of little duration rather than of little content.

Having said that, it is important to recognize the greater value of a "watermelon-size" faith, in contrast to "mustard-seed-size." On the aircraft, although all three of us arrived at our destination at the same time, the man with the greater faith was more relaxed and able to enjoy the journey than the woman with the little faith, or I with the medium faith. It is therefore a legitimate thing to seek an increase of faith, but the only way in which that will come about is by an increase in knowledge of the object of our faith. It is a very simple and obvious principle. The man on the aircraft had presumably flown many times, and with his greater knowledge of air travel was able to be much more confident. Faith in God grows by getting to know God. There is no alternative to that. Paul writes, "Faith comes by hearing and hearing by the word of God" (Rom. 10:17, AV). In the days when Paul wrote that, the average person did not have either the ability to read or access to the Word of God for themselves, so they would hear it read to them as they gathered together for that purpose. The point is that it is through exposure to the Word of God that Christ is revealed to us, and as Christ is revealed to us, we gain a greater understanding and confidence in Him and so are able to trust and exercise faith in Him more readily.

This then is the prime reason for reading the Bible, as we discussed in the previous chapter, that we might know Christ better. Only as we get to know Christ better do we find it easy to trust Him, and the more we get to know Him, the more logical and inevitable it becomes that we trust Him.

As part of the work in which I have been engaged for the past few years, I fly between twenty-five and thirty-five times each year. I am not nervous any more, and, in fact, I am extremely confident. The captain of one aircraft on which I was traveling announced as we landed at our destination, "Ladies and gentlemen, the safest part of your journey is now over. Please drive carefully on the roads." He was right of course. My confidence in aircraft has been born out of experience. The more I have gotten to know and have experienced aircraft, the more I have learned to trust them, even when an engine blows up, as it did on one flight I was on in Canada. There is no substitute for getting to know Christ, and this is the greatest need of our lives, not so that we might hero-worship Him from a distance, but that we might allow Him the freedom to be what He is in our lives and our experience.

So far, all we have done in this chapter is define what faith is. This is valuable only as we go on to discover how it works. Never be satisfied with understanding something, only begin to be satisfied when it has become your experience. Understanding is necessary but I am troubled by the number of Christian people who will discuss, debate, and propagate Christian truths that have never become part of their experience. Doctrine is only valuable as it equips us to live correctly.

10

Obeying What God Says and Trusting Who God Is

In the previous chapter we discussed the nature of faith. Faith is an attitude of trust toward something that enables that something to function in response. If I put faith in a car, I adopt an attitude of trust that enables the car to take me along the road. If I put faith in an aircraft, I adopt an attitude of trust that enables the plane to carry me through the air. If I put faith in a chair, I adopt an attitude of trust in the chair that enables me to sit down and be supported by the chair. In each case, the result of exercising faith is that the object in which the faith has been placed is made free to work on my behalf. Faith is not primarily expressed in what we do, but in what we are trusting the object of our faith to do in response. So it is with God. Faith in God is an attitude of trust in God which enables Him to work.

But how does this work out in practice? What is needed on our part to enable God to work? There are two vital ingredients: *obedience to what God says* and *trust in who God is.*

These two aspects must be understood separately, but they must never be detached from one another. Obedience to the commands of the Lord Jesus Christ without a corresponding trust in Him for the strength and ability those commands require will lead only to frustration and temptations to hypocrisy. If we take the teaching and commands of Jesus seriously without an understanding of His own role in their fulfillment, we can only be discouraged. His commands are humanly impossible. This is why Christendom is such a fertile field for hypocrisy and pretense, as people try desperately hard to obey, but without drawing on the resources of God's strength to fulfill what He commands. On the other hand, to be trusting Christ without a willful and active obedience on our part will lead us into a realm of mysticism that has been known since the seventeenth century as "quietism," which, as the name suggests, is a quiet, passive, wholly subjective resting in God, doing only what one feels constrained and moved by the Spirit to do. Both positions are unhealthy and fall short of what it means to live by faith.

Obedience is an issue at the basis of all genuine Christian experience. The Christian life begins with surrender to and the acknowledgment of the authority of Christ as Lord over our lives. But that initial surrender must be followed by active obedience to the general instruction of Scripture and the particular direction of God over our personal lives. Our experience of the power and sufficiency of God will only be in the context of obedience. God's power is available only for God's purposes.

SAUL, WHO FAILED

Although the word *faith* is hardly used in the Old Testament, the activity of faith runs right through it. Let me illustrate the principle we are talking about by looking at the experience of Saul and David, one who failed and one who succeeded. Saul was the first king over Israel, and when he came to the throne, God made a particular promise about him to Samuel: "He will deliver my people from the hand of the Philistines" (1 Sam. 9:16). The Philistines were a ferocious group of people living to the southwest of Israel, and at that time they were constantly at war with Israel. This was the promise God made about Saul's administration. His role would be fulfilled primarily in military terms.

Saul's initial response to Samuel when told that he would govern the people was a good one. He responded humbly, and after Samuel had anointed him with oil and the Spirit of God had come upon him, he went out and fought the Amalekites who had attacked and humiliated the people of Jabesh Gilead. Having defeated the enemy, he refused the demand of the people to have any of the Amalekites put to death, exclaiming, "for this day the Lord has rescued Israel" (1 Sam. 11:13). Of course, he was right, and he was careful to give the credit to God. The Lord enabled Saul: "the Spirit of the Lord came upon him in power, and he burned with anger" (v. 6). Behind the anger that motivated him and the strength that enabled him was the Spirit of God. Saul started so well. First Samuel 14:47 records, "After Saul had assumed rule over Israel, he fought against their enemies on every side: Moab, the Ammonites, Edom, the kings of

Zobah, and the Philistines. Wherever he turned, he inflicted punishment on them."

However, after such a good start, things began to go badly wrong for Saul. In the forty years that he remained king of Israel he was constantly at war with the Philistines, "All the days of Saul there was bitter war with the Philistines" (1 Sam. 14:52), but apart from the early days of his reign, he lost to them every time. The only two occasions when Israel enjoyed victory was when Jonathan, Saul's son, routed the Philistines (1 Sam. 14), and when David defeated Goliath and sent the Philistine army into retreat (1 Sam. 17). But Saul himself did not experience victory over them, despite it being the promise of God when he was first set apart as king. God's promises are effective only when the conditions for them are being fulfilled, and the fact that He has promised something does not detract from our responsibility to God. Sometimes we hear people talking about "claiming the promises," and it is certainly right to believe them and to take them seriously, but the promises of God are almost always with conditions, and it is the meeting of the conditions that ensure the fulfillment of the promises. It would not have been sufficient for Saul and his men to get together and claim victory over the Philistines. There had to be obedience to God, and there had to be trust in God.

The record of Saul going wrong began with his conflict with the Amalekites (1 Sam. 15). He was given clear instructions by God, but he chose to edit those instructions and to disobey where he disagreed. In the light of his past and his great experiences of God, he began to become familiar with God to the extent that he felt free to pick and choose what he obeyed. We must be very much on guard against experience of God that does not leave us in an attitude of humility and dependence. When God's victories create a self-confidence in us they become dangerous. Many in the Bible and many in history have fizzled into oblivion after such great evidence of blessing, because they became self-sufficient and wrongly interpreted God's victories as their own. Recording the life of King Uzziah, the book of Chronicles states that, "As long as he sought the Lord, God gave him success" (2 Chron. 26:5). It then goes on to record some of his strengths but adds, "he was greatly helped until he became powerful. But after Uzziah became powerful, his pride led to his downfall" (2 Chron. 26:15–16). His experience of God working through him created a self-sufficiency which destroyed him, for he began to rely on his own abilities, not realizing how utterly bankrupt he was apart from God.

When Saul stepped out of a total and unquestioning obedience, the power of God left him. It was Samuel's task to pronounce the verdict on Saul, "Because you have rejected the word of the Lord, he has rejected you as king" (1 Sam. 15:23). The foundation of a life of faith is obedience. Move outside of an obedience to the will of God and you move outside of the resources of God. They simply dry up.

DAVID, WHO SUCCEEDED

In sharp contrast to Saul's failure, there is the record of the victories of his successor, David—not that David was without his failings. The Bible is disarmingly honest about the failings of its greatest characters, and the record of David is no exception. But David was a man who proved again and again the adequacy of God to fulfill all of His own demands and to bring into reality all the promises He had made.

Perhaps the best example of this, and the one which most clearly illustrates the principle of living by faith, is found in David's battle with Goliath. David was still a young man, probably only a teenager, although he had already been anointed by Samuel in anticipation of his becoming king over Israel. He was too young to join the army, remaining at home to tend his father's sheep while his brothers went away to fight. However, sent by his father to deliver some grain, bread, and cheese to his brothers, he arrived at the scene of the battle in the Valley of Elah only to discover the army sitting in their tents "dismayed and terrified" and no battle taking place. The reason was that for almost six weeks now, every morning and again in the evening, Goliath had stepped from the Philistine camp asking for a challenger from Israel to take him on. He had proposed that one member of the Israelite army should battle with one member of the Philistine army, and the winner of that battle would be the winner of the whole war. If the Philistine won, then Israel would bow to the Philistines. If the Israelite won, then the Philistines would bow to the Israelites. It was certainly an intriguing way to fight a war and would cut down on the excessive bloodshed. For reasons best known only to himself, Saul, as king of Israel, accepted the challenge. Goliath presented himself as the Philistine who would have to be fought. He was just over nine feet tall. His armor alone weighed about one hundred and twenty-five pounds, and just the iron point of his spear weighed fifteen pounds!

Across in the Israelite camp no volunteer came forward to accept the challenge. For forty days, twice each day, Goliath came forward to meet a representative of the Israelite army to fight the duel. But there was no one. The most obvious opponent in the Israelite camp was Saul, for he is described as being "head and shoulders above the rest." But like the others, he cowered in his tent for those forty days, "dismayed and terrified." Twice each day, eighty times in all, they had been humiliated by the roar across the valley from Goliath asking for a soldier, and twice each day, "When the Israelites saw the man, they all ran from him in great fear" (1 Sam. 17:24). Saul tried to bribe a volunteer into going to meet Goliath. First he offered great wealth. That received no takers, probably in the realization that if one fought and lost—which was likely—great wealth wouldn't be much use, other than to pay for a fancy funeral—that was assuming there was something left to bury. Next, Saul offered his daughter in marriage to the man who would fight. Finally, Saul announced that not just the man who fights, but his whole family, brothers, sisters, the lot, would be exempt from taxes in Israel for the rest of their lives. I am sure some families pricked up their ears at this and immediately nominated some unfortunate member of the family to go and fight, so that even if he lost, the rest would become exempt from tax for the rest of their days. However, no one was persuaded to actually take up the challenge.

It was at this stage, forty days into the dilemma, that David arrived on the scene with the food for his brothers. I can well imagine the conversation that took place when David reached them.

"Why are you not fighting this morning?"

"We have a problem."

"What is the problem?"

"Goliath!"

"I beg your pardon?"

"Goliath!"

"Who is Goliath?"

"He is the big brute across the valley, shouting at the top of his lungs. No, no, not that. That's an oak tree. The one next to it!"

"Why is he a problem?"

"He has put out a challenge to someone in the Israelite army to go and fight him, and whoever wins that fight, wins the war."

"Why is that a problem?"

"Because he is big! Very big! V. . . v. . . very, v. . . very b . . . b . . . big!"

"I can see he is big, but you haven't answered my question. Why is that a problem?"

"There is no one on this side who is capable of handling him."

"But isn't God on your side? Goliath is not just defying the Israelite army, he is defying God. God has promised that the Philistine army will be defeated and that Israel will be delivered from their oppression. It is not you he is challenging, but God!"

"David, don't be so spiritual about these things. We all know God is on our side, but we have to be practical about these things too, you know. It is all very well you coming in and being simplistic and spiritual about the answer, but we have to be realistic. In any case, we know what God's promise is, and we have claimed it, and we hold early morning prayer meetings too. In fact, next Friday we are having a half night of prayer about it. We know how conceited you are, David, you only came down here to watch the battle and get a good view of some fighting. Well, there is nothing going on, so go back home to your sheep."

With that they sent him away. But "he turned away to someone else and brought up the same matter, and the men answered the same as before" (1 Sam. 17:30). Eventually he came to Saul and made the promise, "Let no one lose heart on account of this Philistine; your servant will go and fight him." Saul objected, pointing out that David was only a boy and that Goliath had been a fighting man from his youth. David was insistent, and on reflection, Saul probably realized that sooner or later something had to happen. When it did, it would almost certainly mean humiliation and defeat for Israel, and considering it a better investment to lose a boy than to lose a soldier, he agreed to let him go.

Just pause at this stage. What is "living by faith" in this context? Was it simply claiming the promise that God would deliver them from the Philistines? Was it holding prayer meetings for Goliath's defeat? After all, God could work a miracle and give him a heart attack or some kind of cerebral hemorrhage or even better, just strike him dead without any obvious symptoms! They could have gotten together and said, "Let us believe God for that." No, what they needed was someone who would obey what God had said and trust who God is.

God was not going to work outside of their obedience or prove anything in advance of their obedience. If Goliath was going to fall, someone would have to act in unreserved obedience followed by unreserved trust.

We will rarely see God at work unless we are prepared to take risks. I do not mean to take wild risks in which we go beyond what God has said and test Him in some way, but risks in which in sheer obedience we step into seemingly impossible situations and rely upon only one fact: That God has told us to go, and therefore God will take the consequences. As Major Ian Thomas has said, "Do not ask if something is possible. Only ask if it is right." If we live only in the realm of the possible all the time there will be little adventure and little to be excited about. But if we are prepared to seek what is right and then do it, even though it may be against overwhelming odds, we will see God come into action and work miracles that leave us thrilled and humbled.

The question of what was possible did not occupy David for very long. He thought about it and remembered that the Lord had delivered him when he fought a lion and when he fought a bear attacking his father's sheep. One of the great encouragements about allowing God to work in our lives is that every time we do so, we have experience of His faithfulness to look back on, which makes it easier the next time.

The issue most important to David was what was right. If he was doing what was right, God would look after the consequences. Declining Saul's armor, for it was far too big anyway, David went off to meet Goliath. Saul piously and insincerely sent him off with the right words, "Go, and the Lord be with you" (v. 37). What a person will believe about God's readiness to work in and through someone else is never the test of what one believes about God. We all believe in the great God who worked so effectively in people like Hudson Taylor, C. T. Studd, George Müller, or D. L. Moody, but we do not believe in the sufficiency of the same God in us. We will rejoice over stories of God working through our contemporaries, too, and acknowledge the good things that have been done. But it is what we believe about God in our own lives that reflects what we really believe about God. If Saul believed the "God be with you" that he uttered to David, he would have gone himself forty days earlier.

As David descended the Israelite side of the Valley of Elah, I imagine a great hush coming over the Israelite camp as they watched him go. David's brothers were wondering how they were going to explain this to their father. He had only come to bring them food, and here he is, going onto the battlefield to face someone whom none of the professional soldiers dared face. He was surely going to be slaughtered! Some of the big men like Saul would have felt a twinge of guilt as this young, small teenager went to do the job they should have been prepared to do. The Philistines, too, wondered at the spectacle, and Goliath took it as an insult. "Am I dog that you come against me with sticks?" he bawled.

David's reply revealed the secret of his boldness. "You come against me with sword and spear and javelin, but I come against you in the name of the Lord Almighty, the God of the armies of Israel, whom you have defied. This day the Lord will hand you over to me, and I'll strike you down and cut off your head. Today I will give the carcasses of the Philistine army to the birds of the air and the beasts of the earth, and the whole world will know that there is a God in Israel. All those gathered here will know that it is not by sword or spear that the Lord saves; for the battle is the Lord's, and he will give all of you into our hands" (v. 45–47). With that, David ran to meet him, and reaching into his bag he took out one of five smooth stones, placed it in his sling, took careful aim, and slung the stone, striking Goliath on the forehead. The Scripture graphically records, "The stone sank into his forehead, and he fell face down on the ground" (v. 49).

TRUST AND OBEY

That story reminds us of Sunday school days. We love stories of heroes, and this is one of the most exciting. But the principles by which David lived his life in this event are intended to be the principles by which you and I live our lives. This is not a story to be relegated to moments of escapism and fantasy, but it is the record of how a child of God became a man of God. David experienced victory because he did two things that any one of the Israelite soldiers could have done. He obeyed what God said, first of all. He knew the will of God in the situation, and he stepped out, took what appeared to be an enormous human risk, and he obeyed. He did what he knew to be right, even though it meant stepping out alone. But obedience has to be accompanied by trust. David trusted God to be totally sufficient for victory. The secret was not in his slingshot ability, though he certainly knew how to handle his sling, but in his God who had called him to the situation and who accomplished His purposes through him. I repeat, David proved the adequacy of God in the context of his obedience to God, and without his initiative in obeying, he would never have seen the Lord work through him.

Is this why some Christians and some churches never give much evidence of a God who lives and works? Are they too afraid to take what appear to be big risks in stepping out where God has told them to go, holding prayer meetings for the work instead of actually doing it? Praying is important, of course, but it can become an escape route from obedience if we refuse to obey God and to get on with the responsibilities He has called us to fulfill.

Interestingly, as soon as Goliath fell to the ground, the Israelite army left its tents, bounded down the hill, and pursued the fleeing Philistines to the gates of the city of Gath. The church will jump on the bandwagon of other people's victories and enjoy the benefits of them. When a man proves God in a big way and experiences God doing marvelous things, we love to hear about it, talk about it, and read about it, but are often not prepared to pay the price ourselves. The Israelites even wrote songs about David, one of which became a great dancing song, with the words, "Saul has killed his thousands, and David his tens of thousands" (see 1 Sam. 21:11). Yet all the time they sang the songs about David and retold the story about David, they probably forgot that there had been a forty-day opportunity for any one of those fighting men to have proved the same thing themselves.

Saddest of all, not only did Saul not experience the victory of God himself, but when David came along and was prepared to do so, Saul became jealous. After Saul had first heard the "Saul has slain his thousands, and David his tens of thousands" song, the Bible records, "Saul was very angry. . . . And from that time on Saul kept a jealous eye on David" (1 Sam. 18:8–9). When a Christian will not let God be God in his own experience, he will always begin to dislike those who will. We will make heroes of men and women like this provided they are in history books or live a long way from us, but there is little the superficial Christian will like less than someone close whose godliness and activity exposes his or her own failure to take God really seriously and let Him be God. Although David defeated one enemy in the Valley of Elah, he was actually creating more. And many of them were among God's own people.

People who should know better will often become jealous when others begin to make advances with God—especially if they are younger. But for David, becoming an enemy of the most powerful man in the nation was part of the price of being obedient.

The tragedy of Saul's life was that although the promises of God were known to him and he had past experience of the faithfulness of God in fulfilling His promises, he began to pick and choose when to obey. Because his obedience was erratic, God's provision appeared to him to be erratic, for His provision is only available for His plans. When a person steps out of God's plans, he will not experience God's adequacy. This was Saul's problem. He now had a history of failure as well as the success of his early days, and rather than face up to the fact that he was the cause of the failure through his pride and disobedience, he doubted the sufficiency of God. Faced with Goliath, he knew what he should do, but unlike David, he had a history of only selective obedience that had deprived himself of learning how consistently God is wholly trustworthy.

Do you live by faith? This is what David has been illustrating for us. It has to do with your obedience to God and your trust in God, for these two must never be detached. It has to do with recognizing Christ as your Lord, and realizing Him as your life. Whatever God has given you to do and will give you to do, He is totally adequate for. You will not prove that sitting in the church, studying in the classroom, or reading this book. You may learn the principles in this way, but the laboratory in which this will be made real in your experience will be your Valley of Elah, with a giant against whom you have no reasonable hope of victory were you to meet him on your own, but with the promise of God behind you and the life of God within you, step out and enjoy a display of the glory and goodness of God! You will pay for it, as David paid when he became a fugitive on the run from Saul for many years, but it was worth it.

It does not mean that every day is going to be comfortable, or every story is going to be triumphant, for there are times God will lead you into circumstances for which He will give you no explanation, and at times you will be involved in events for which you do not see the significance, but "we live by faith, not by sight" (2 Cor. 5:7), and God does not have to keep explaining Himself.

11

In Christ and into Action

God not only has plans *for* this world, but He also has plans *in* this world. Every new day brings its outworking of the purposes of God. But how are they accomplished? The remarkable answer is that His purposes are primarily accomplished through people, and what is more, through very ordinary people. When I was a young Christian, I believed that there were certain special people that God liked to use and through whom He liked to work. There were those whose lives were characterized by a freshness and vitality that drew others to Christ, and the best someone like me could contribute would be praying for those whom God was using, listening to them, encouraging them, and supporting them, but I could not expect the same God to work through me. I had wrongly concluded that the plans of God passed the ordinary person by. He or she had to keep the basic rules, but other than that was left on the sidelines only to observe and admire. The truth is that the ordinary person is intended by Jesus Christ to be the very vehicle of His working, for He has chosen that the particular means of expressing Himself to people is through other people. God has no special favorites. He is willing to work through any person who is willing to let Him.

Although it is true that God's plans are people, it is, in itself, an inadequate statement concerning His strategy in the world. A more accurate statement would be to say that His plan is Christ. God has no plans outside of Jesus Christ, and we share in the outworking of those plans by virtue of being "in Christ." It is our union with Him that qualifies us for participation in His strategy. I want to explore, in this last chapter, what this statement means for you and me as individuals.

When a person becomes a Christian, there are two things that take place in his or her experience—Christ comes to live in the person, and the person comes to live in Christ. We have already said much about Christ being in us, but it is equally important to understand what it means for us to be in Christ. Although this particular expression is unique in the New Testament to the writings of Paul, it is nevertheless the most frequent description that he does use when speaking of the relationship between the believer and the Lord Jesus Christ. Outside of Paul's writings, if the actual expression "in Christ" is not found, the idea can still be seen.

On the day of Pentecost, a large crowd of people responded to the preaching of Peter, and the book of Acts records that "there were added that day about three thousand souls" (Acts 2:41). This is an interesting expression. The original text does not specify as to what this great crowd was added, although some translations use expressions like, "added to their number," in an attempt to make what may seem to be a slightly obscure statement make sense. However, later in the book of Acts the same words are used with the added qualification that many were "added to the Lord" (Acts 5:14 and 11:24, AV). These people who had responded to the preaching of the Gospel were not just added to an organization or to some religious club, but they were added to the Lord Himself. In a real and marvelous way they became incorporated into Jesus Christ so that their identity became intimately associated with His identity.

Paul later describes the church as being "the body of Christ" and that "we were all baptized by one Spirit into one body—whether Jews or Greeks, slaves or free—and we were all given the one Spirit to drink" (1 Cor. 12:13). This union with Christ is such that the church is described as being His body, the actual physical being through which His life and His purposes are to be expressed and accomplished. I am sure it is not necessary for me to stress that the church in the New Testament is not a building or an organization, but it is men, women, young people, children, from every background and color of skin who, upon repentance of their sin and faith in the Lord Jesus Christ, have become indwelt by His Spirit and incorporated into His body. The church is not an organization but an organism, a living unit, the members being united together by the indwelling life of Jesus Christ. It is the sharing together of His life that makes us part of His body.

THE VALUE OF A BODY
In order to understand the truth of the church being the body of Christ, think about your own physical body for a moment. Your

body is not you, it is only the place where you live. The apostle Paul describes it as " the earthly tent we live in" (2 Cor. 5:1), which may not be the most complimentary description of the shape of some bodies, but which nevertheless illustrates the truth that the physical bodies we possess only house the real person. Were you to lose both of your legs and both of your arms, you would lose about half of your body but would be as much the actual person as you were before. You would not be able to function as well, but you would be as fully the same person as before.

I remember being in the home of an elderly woman who had just died; I was expressing my condolences to the family regarding her having "passed away" when I was asked if I would like to see her! I didn't wish to, but was struck with the incongruity of having talked about her having passed away in one breath and about "seeing her" in the next. It would sound a contradiction to speak of seeing someone who has just gone. The truth of course was that the real person had passed away, but she had left her body behind, which was waiting to be taken away. The person is not the body, and the body is not the person.

This is true of you, and this is true of Christ. Your body is your home, but it is not you. The church is the home of the Lord Jesus Christ, but it is not He Himself. However, having said that, your body is very important to you, for everything that you do, you do with your body. When you go to work, you work with your body. When you relax and play a game or watch a film, you do so with your body. Every ambition you hold will involve your body for its fulfillment. The body is the means whereby the real you, who lives within it, is able to be expressed, through which your thoughts are spoken, your plans fulfilled, and your work done. Without a body none of these things would take place.

On occasions when I am going to preach somewhere, a friend may get in touch and say, "I am sorry I will not be able to be with you today, but be assured, I will be with you in spirit." Whenever someone says that, I am grateful for the sentiment, but I am careful not to ask them to open in prayer or sing a solo for that meeting! To be present in spirit yet without a body (if that were possible) does not leave you capable of very much. There is great value in a body. In fact, bodies are absolutely necessary if we are going to get things done.

Jesus Christ has great plans for this world, and He has created a means of accomplishing them. It is a body—a body in which He is to live and through which He is to speak His thoughts, fulfill His plans, and perform His work. It is not the single body He once lived in as He spent His thirty-three earthly years in and around Israel, but it is a new body given to Him on the Day of Pentecost, which was its birthday. On that day not only did the disciples receive new life, which was nothing less than His life, but He received a new body. He received new hands to work with—their hands. He received new feet to walk with—their feet. He received new lips to speak with—their lips. He received new hearts to love with—their hearts.

From then on, the same Lord Jesus Christ who had worked for the years of His earthly life in His one body would continue to do His work through a new body, the church. He would be its Head and its life, but the physical means of His work being done would be through the lives and bodies of His members who were to be made available to Him for this purpose. This is the theme of the book of Acts. When Luke introduces the book of Acts he says, "In my former book, Theophilus, I wrote about all that Jesus began to do and to teach" (Acts 1:1). When we read his former book, Luke's Gospel, we discover a record of the whole of Jesus' life and work, concluding with His ascension to the Father in heaven. But Luke describes that as being only a record of "all that Jesus began to do and to teach," the implication being that his second volume, the book of Acts, is a record of all that this same Lord Jesus Christ continued to do and to teach, not now through His single body, but through His new body which is the church, given to Him at Pentecost. This was the effect of Pentecost from God's point of view, for it was the creation of a new body which would become the vehicle through which the life, character, activity, and purposes of Jesus Christ would be expressed and accomplished.

It is important for us to understand this from God's point of view. Paul said to the Ephesians, "I pray also that the eyes of your heart may be enlightened in order that you may know the hope to which he has called you, the riches of *his glorious inheritance* in the saints" (Eph. 1:18). It is good to rejoice in "our inheritance," and Paul writes about that earlier in the same chapter, "Having believed, you were marked in him with a seal, the promised Holy Spirit, who is a deposit guaranteeing our inheritance until the redemption of those who are God's possession" (Eph. 1:13–14), but we need to see beyond "our inheritance" and try to understand what is "his glorious inheritance in the saints." We are not the only beneficiaries in our salvation. Remarkable as it may seem, God is a beneficiary too. Paul's prayer for the Ephesians is that they may understand and appreciate what God has inherited in them, and so cease their tendencies to selfishness in their Christian lives by being only concerned with what they receive in Him, but may seek to bring to fulfillment all that Christ has received in them.

The characteristics that make the church Christ's body are the same characteristics that make your flesh and bones your body. It comes into being as the domicile of your life and operates under the direction of your head. Similarly, Paul speaks to the Ephesians about the fact that corporately, "You too are being built together to become a dwelling in which God lives by his Spirit" (Eph. 2:22), and they are to function "under one head, even Christ" (Eph. 1:10).

Before we discuss the practical expression of the life of Christ through His church, I want to make absolutely clear that this is all part and parcel of becoming a Christian and not something additional that may be added later. The event of Christ's coming to live within us and we coming to be in Him must be a simultaneous event. Let me illustrate this by one of the recent marvels of modern medicine—microsurgery. Microsurgery is the process whereby severed fingers, arms, or legs are stitched back into place so that they are able to function as near to normal as possible. As I write this, it is about a year since a particularly fascinating example of this surgery was given considerable publicity in the news media in England. A farmer had been bailing up some loose straw in one of his fields when his machine jammed. Seeing what was wrong, he dismounted the tractor, leaving the machinery running. He put his hand into the bailer to remove the cause of the problem, which he managed to do effectively. However, as he did so, his arm got caught, pulled into the machine, and was severed in a clean cut above the elbow. He then had the presence of mind to pick up the severed arm in his other hand and walk one-third of a mile to the nearest house. Upon getting there, he knocked on the door (I am not sure which hand he used!), and the woman in the house telephoned for an ambulance. In the meantime she packed his arm in all the available ice she could get from her deep freeze and refrigerator. The ambulance arrived, took the man and his arm to the hospital, and during lengthy surgery the arm was painstakingly stitched back into place. Several months later I saw a photograph in a newspaper of the man back at work, his arm not fully functioning as yet, but the prognosis was that it would eventually be restored to normal use. Similar events have made newsworthy stories in recent months, and I can recall incidents of individuals having a severed hand, a leg, or one man who lost both of his feet in an attempted suicide, all having their limbs reattached and restored to their normal function.

Now go back to the farmer. When his arm was replaced, two things happened simultaneously. The arm received the life of the body, and at the same time the body received the arm. When the arm had been severed, it was lifeless. You could tickle its palm and get no response. You could tread on its thumb and it would not react. To all intents and purposes it was dead.

This of course is the condition you and I are described as being in apart from Christ, "dead in your transgressions and sins" (Eph. 2:1). As the arm was reattached to the body, the success of the operation was measured by the return of the life to the arm. The life returned to the arm at the precise moment that the arm was returned to the body, for the life in the arm was the life of the body. The hospital staff, despite their great skill, could not put life into the arm first, as a separate operation, while the rest of the man sat outside in the waiting room having a cup of tea, then, having successfully gotten the arm to come alive, call him in and stitch the living arm back onto the body. Could you imagine a living arm lying on the table, flexing its wrist, clenching its fist, pointing with its finger, or rolling around on its own, but detached from the body? It would be impossible! In the same way, spiritual new birth cannot be detached from our baptism by the Spirit into Christ. The impartation of His life to us is simultaneous with the incorporation of our lives into His body. We become His body at the same time that He becomes our life. The two events cannot be separated.

GOD WILL USE YOU

There are many ways that God works out His will and purposes, but the primary means of His working among people is through the church. All that we do personally is done through our bodies, and all that the Lord Jesus Christ is doing among people is through His body, the church. He has chosen it to be that way, and therefore we do not expect Him to work outside His church or apart from His church but through His church. I do not know how you personally may have come to know Christ, except for one thing. There was some human agency involved. Perhaps you listened to someone preaching the Gospel, and through such means the Holy Spirit convicted you of your need and of the sufficiency of Christ to meet that need. Perhaps you read a book that someone had written or you read the Bible which was written by men under the inspiration of the Holy Spirit, and as a result you came to know Christ. It could be that in your place of work or study or as you observed a neighbor, you saw a life that was so different that it created an appetite to seek for what he or she so obviously had, and you discovered it was Christ. Whatever the cause, somewhere along the line, God used people to speak to you about Himself. I am quite sure that you were not just walking along the road one day when suddenly an angel appeared in front of you, placed his wings behind his back and said, "Excuse me, I would like to talk to you about Christ." Wouldn't it be wonderful if God chose to work that way? Don't you think it would be very convincing? In fact, God has thousands of angels just waiting for an opportunity to obey Him. In His sovereignty and wisdom God is perfectly free to send angels to do His work, and there are times when He does, but His general means of working on earth is through His own body, which is the church, which is people, which is you and me.

If God has worked through others to reach you, His plan is that He might now work through you to reach others. That is an obvious statement in the light of all we have been thinking about. Serving the Lord Jesus Christ is not an optional extra to the Christian life but is an inevitable part of the relationship with Christ into which we have been brought. Remember that it is His purpose to express Himself through His body the church, and therefore not to be concerned with serving Him will involve deliberate disobedience to the One under whose authority we have willingly placed ourselves. This is a vital part of being a Christian. I have heard it suggested more than once that if a Christian does not take advantage of the opportunities God gives him to serve that He will send someone else along instead. I am not at all sure about that. I do not think that God has a lot of Christians waiting on the sidelines to step into the place of a disobedient Christian. Jesus said to His disciples, "The harvest is plentiful but the workers are few" (Matt. 9:37). In other words, there is always more to be done than there are people willing to do it.

Ezekiel records an occasion in the Old Testament when God said, "I looked for a man among them who would build up the wall and stand before me in the gap on behalf of the land so I would not have to destroy it, but I found none. Therefore I will pour out my wrath on them and consume them with my fiery anger, bringing down on their heads all they have done, declares the Sovereign Lord" (Ezek. 22:30–31). God states there that because He could not find a man through whom He could work, the work did not get done, and He was left with no option but to pour out His wrath. God is not outwitted by our disobedience, but the principle is that He has chosen to work through people and not to bypass people.

Some years ago I first heard the fable built around the time of Jesus' ascension to heaven. It is, of course, only a fable, and I hesitate to quote it, but its message is so appropriate to what I am trying to say. In the fable, as Jesus returned to heaven all the angels gathered around Him, welcoming Him back after His thirty-three-year absence while on earth. They ask Him about His time as a Man, how people reacted to Him, and He tells of His initial popularity and then rejection and crucifixion, followed by His resurrection from the dead. In the forty days since then, He explained, He had spent time with eleven men, giving them proofs of His resurrection and teaching them about the kingdom of God. One of the angels is reported in the fable to have asked, "Now that You have returned to heaven, what are Your plans?" to which Jesus is said to reply, "I have left just those eleven men behind to carry on the work."

"Just eleven men!" exclaimed an angel. "What happens if they fail?" Jesus is said to reply, "If those eleven men fail, I have no other plans." I do not believe the fable, but I believe the statement. Of course, those men were to be filled with the Holy Spirit, but nevertheless, it was to be through them that the work of the Lord Jesus Christ would continue. They didn't fail! That is why we are here today.

One of the lies of the Devil is to create the assumption in the thinking of many Christians that "God can't use me." We recognize His ability to use other people but do not expect it for ourselves, and thereby we not only grieve the Holy Spirit, but we miss what is surely the greatest adventure in life.

A few years ago I was invited to be the "padre" at a boys' camp attended by something like one hundred boys, aged from twelve to sixteen. We were camping in the field, and the boys slept in groups of ten in smaller tents that encircled the large tent in which we ate and held a daily meeting. For the last half hour of the day, each group of ten would meet with their "tent officer" for what we called a "Quiet Time." They would review the day's activities, talk about what they had learned, perhaps have a Bible reading and time of prayer before (theoretically) going to sleep. One evening, while the Quiet Time was taking place, I was talking to one of the other leaders in the main tent when suddenly one of the tent officers came bursting in through the door.

"Are you free for a few minutes?" he asked me. "There is a boy in my tent who says he would like to become a Christian. I have been talking to him about it through the day, and I have just asked him if he would be prepared to give himself to Christ, and he says he would."

"Then why have you come to get me?" I asked.

"Because you are the padre at this camp!"

"That doesn't mean I am a spiritual midwife," I responded. "Why don't you lead him to Christ yourself?"

"I have never done that before," he explained, "and I wouldn't know what to say."

"But you never will lead anyone to Christ if every time you have the opportunity you go and look for someone else. You have been talking to him all day, you tell me. Of course you know what to say!" I then suggested that rather than I go and speak with him, he should go back and speak to him alone, while we stayed in the tent and prayed for them. He wasn't at all keen on the idea, and suggested that he would come and listen to anything I might say to the boy, and next time he had the opportunity, he would try to bring someone to the point of commitment himself. I had begun to feel very strongly that I should not go and talk to the boy and told the tent officer this, but promised that we would pray for him instead. He protested, but eventually went. About half an hour later he came running back into the main tent. "You will never guess what happened," he shouted to us.

"How many guesses do we have?" I asked him.

"One," he replied.

"He became a Christian," I told him. He sat down and explained how he had told the boy what was involved in surrendering his life to Christ. As the boy indicated his willingness for this, they had prayed together and he asked Christ to become the Lord and Master of his life. "It was so fantastic," the tent officer said to us, and then added, "Do you mind if I cry?"

During that week that same fellow led two or three other boys to Christ. In his several years as a Christian he had made the assumption that God would not use him in the way he knew He could use others. At that camp a new appetite was kindled, to get off the sidelines and into the action, and he began to enjoy a new adventure in life. God could use him and God would use him.

This privilege belongs to you too. It is true that God will use different people in different ways, and none of us will be used in identical ways. But the principle is so important to grasp, that no matter what I may think of myself and my capabilities, the Lord Jesus Christ has invited me to become part of His body and the means through which He does His work. We must not just commit ourselves to the work but to the Head of the body, so that He can direct us to fulfill whatever He has planned.

When Jesus told His disciples that "The harvest is plentiful but the workers are few," His instructions which followed on the basis of that statement were not, "Go therefore and evangelize as much as you can," but "Ask the Lord of the harvest, therefore, to send out workers into his harvest field" (Matt. 9:38). They were not to run off and do as much as they possibly could, but to be in touch with the "Lord of the harvest" so that He could direct them to whomever He might choose whenever He might choose. The Lord is the strategist, and He alone knows where He wants us to be and what He wants us to do.

In the Acts of the Apostles, the apostles and leaders of the early church were not committed to a strategy, but to Christ. Any strategy that derived from the Lord was good, but their commitment was to Him. In Acts 8, the Gospel has spread to Samaria, through the ministry of Philip in particular. There followed one of the greatest responses to Christ anywhere outside of Jerusalem, and Philip was the main leader and preacher. However, the record states, "Now an angel of the Lord said to Philip, 'Go south to the road—the desert road—that goes down from Jerusalem to Gaza.' So he started out" (Acts 8:26–27). How would you respond in such circumstances? Philip is being marvelously used of God in preaching to the huge crowds that gathered in Samaria when he receives instructions to leave and go to a desert road! No one lives on the desert road. He is being taken away from an opportunity for large-scale evangelism. But Philip "started out, and on his way he met an Ethiopian eunuch" and you may know the rest of the story, how Philip led this man to

Christ, baptized him, and sent him on his way to Ethiopia to introduce the Gospel to that part of Africa. Philip was committed to Jesus Christ, not just to evangelism. Had he dedicated himself to being a great evangelist, he would not have left Samaria.

God does not want us to be dedicated primarily to causes, but to be available to Christ. He may call us to give our lives in the interest of some particular cause, but our commitment is primarily to Christ, and consequently, to anything He has given us to do. Every new morning we can anticipate that the Lord Jesus Christ will be free to express Himself through us that day and accomplish some aspect of His work, whether we can identify what He has done or not. This is our privilege, and this is our responsibility.

For Christ to be in us gives us *power*. We can live effectively in no other strength than that which derives from the life of Jesus Christ, for He said, "Apart from me you can do nothing" (John 15:5). And for us to be in Christ gives us *purpose*. It is not a power that enables us to live for ourselves, but it equips us to fulfill the plans of Christ who is the Head of the body.

For Christ to be in us gives us *resources*. Everything we possibly need is ours in the Lord Jesus Christ. And for us to be in Christ gives us *responsibilities*. As part of His body, the most important issue I have to face is, "What do you want me to do?"

For Christ to be in us is *dynamic*. And for us to be in Christ is *demanding*. If He has something to do, He has the right to use us as the means of doing it. If there is an "Ethiopian eunuch" on the desert road, He has the right to tell you to leave your Samaria and go to meet him. But for every demand He makes, He provides the dynamic of His Spirit within to accomplish it.

This is the Christian life. Having faced our failure to express His likeness and image in the world, we come to the Cross for forgiveness, are indwelt by the Holy Spirit, and become incorporated into Christ, to become vehicles for the expression of His life and purpose. The world desperately needs to know this but will have no grounds on which to believe it until they see the life and character of Jesus Christ lived out in your life and mine. This is God's purpose for you! It was His purpose when He first created man and is therefore the only thing that makes life make sense in any ultimate way. Have you found reality in Jesus Christ, or have you substituted something else?